Joanne Sigler Remembers When

Reminicences of Shreveport, Louisiana of the 1930s-50s

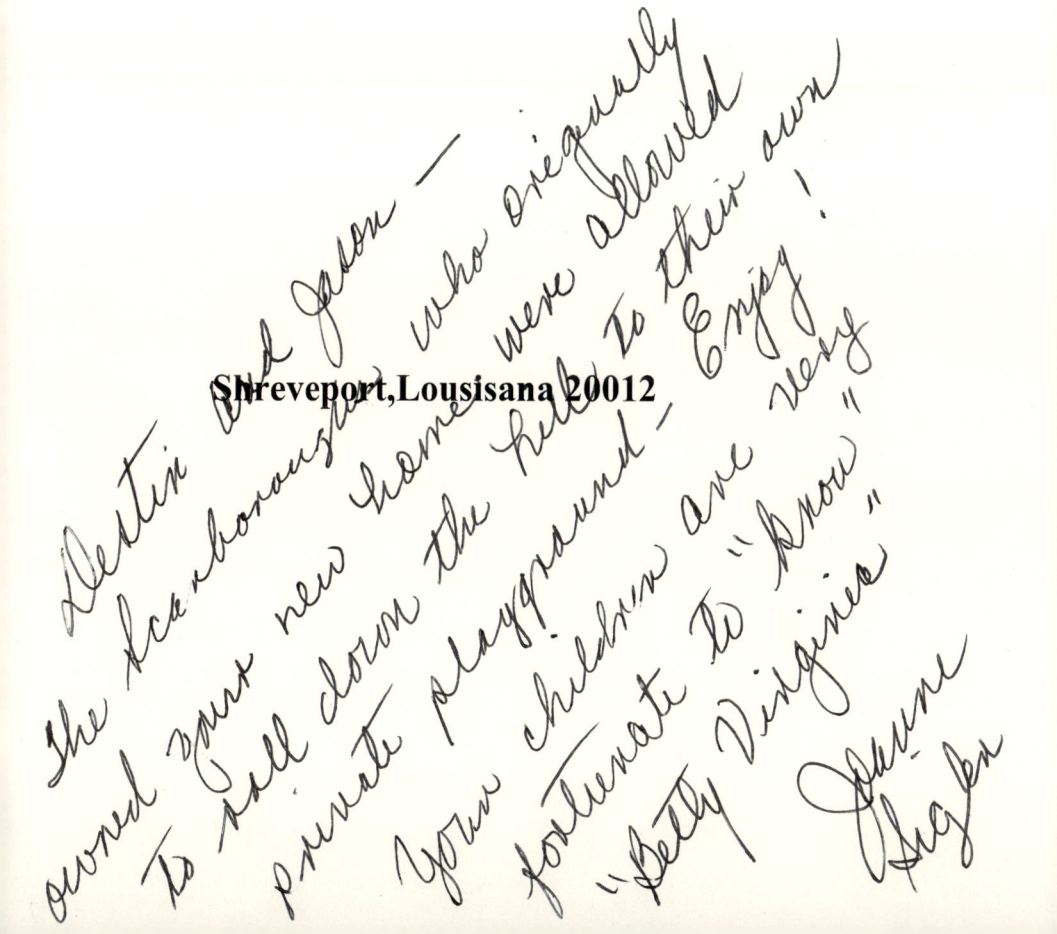

Shreveport, Lousisana 20012

*Destin and Jason —
The Scarboroughs, who originally owned your new home, were allowed to sill down the hill to their own private playground — Enjoy! Your children are very fortunate to "know" "Betty Virginia"*

Joanne Sigler

Introduction

Remember growing up in Shreveport? We had a relatively quiet and sheltered life. We enjoyed all the children's games, the p'like adventures, and the discipline on all levels. Enduring the four years of war we learned many lessons about ourselves before graduating from the 7th grade. We were on our way to C.E. Byrd High School or Fair Park High School. How all the seventh graders of all the elementary schools squeezed into those buildings I'll never know ... but we did.

Naturally we lived in our own neighborhoods, venturing out to Church, Sunday School, and to visit relatives. Following the war we still were concerned with the lack of gasoline and other restrictions. Hence we more or less remained in our respective neighborhood. There were no distinguishing signs marking the limits of a nieghborhood, we knew our limitations of walking and bicycle riding.

When we arrived at high school a whole new world was opened to each of us. We met new friends, visited in their homes, met them downtown, attended their birthday parties and visited their churches and synagogues, and especially exchanging telephone numbers!

That was when my life began, I didn't want to miss a single thing. Every new experience was shared with Mother, Daddy and Kiki. I didn't keep a diary because there wasn't time. The war was over in October after I started to Byrd.Life was beautiful for everyone I knew. We had fun, played hard, minded our parents, still cleaned our plates and wanted to absorb life every waking moment.

I've tried to shake my memory bank in order to share those days of the late 30's, 40's and 50' s and bring you up to the present. It has been said that "the impact of the past on present and future memories is what made us form our ideas and ideals of today. "I would like to encourage you to remember and cherish your past and appreciate the influence people and events have made on each of our lives."

MEMORIES OF PARKS

Parks –

    Definition: a. A piece of ground in or near a city or town kept for recreation. b. An area maintained in its natural state as a public property. c. A respite in which to relax, reflect, rejuvenate, and really have a wonderful time.

    A and B are according to Webster, C is according to me. The word itself sends a warm feeling to my mind and heart. Having spent many hours playing in parks I treasure all those memories especially the swings. Remember Robert Louis Stevenson's poem?

> How do you like to go up in a swing,
>   Up in the air so blue?
> Oh, I do think it the pleasantest thing
>   Ever a child can do!
>
> Up in the air and over the wall,
>   Till I can see so wide,
> Rivers and trees and cattle and all
>   Over the countryside –
>
> Till I look down on the garden green,
>   Down on the roof so brown –
> Up in the air I go flying again,
>   Up in the air and down.

    How many times have I heard my mother repeat those words when she was pushing me in my own swing at home or in the park swing?

    I can still feel the wind in my face and through my hair as I would "pump" in order to get higher and then reverse the direction and lean way back and look up at the sky for flying birds hoping I could match their speed only to start "pumping" again – back and forth, back and forth. What a life! I still like to swing.

My childhood friend Peggy and I would take turns trying to outdo each other. 60 years later Peggy gave me a bronze statue of a little girl on a swing. What a grand reminder of fun times, summer days, and a beautiful friendship.

Swings and parks just seem to be the most tranquilizing synonyms I can think of. I believe my early fascination of parks began when my parents began telling me about Princess Park. As I was growing up we would drive by it quite often on our trip to downtown Shreveport.

My parents met soon after mother graduated from Shreveport High School in 1920. As you can probably understand, entertainment was limited. Saturday nights were designated as the night to board the streetcar and go to Princess Park where music was played from the bandstand and people danced and picnicked. Can't you imagine the scene there at the corner of Fairfield and Common Street? For my parents it must have been magic! They married in 1923 so I'm sure there were many Saturday nights enjoying Princess Park.

Growing up in Shreveport in the 30's and 40's, my park, Thomas Field, played an important part in my life. It was located on Southern Avenue across the street from Uncle Joe's Bottling Company in Sunny Slope Subdivision. There were wonder swings, a tennis court, rings, a trapeze, a huge slide and a brick pavilion. It was a perfect place for birthday parties, school parties, family picnics, or for just a couple of hours – what else was there to do???

One important event was that the City Recreation Department would announce in the Shreveport Times when movies would be shown in the different parks in the city. A projector and screen would be set up along with a popcorn machine, the Popsicle man, snow cones, and the ice cream man who brought Dixie cups with movie star's pictures on the lids. Families would appear with blankets, picnic baskets, flashlights, and enough enthusiasm to drive parents absolutely crazy. You just had to be there! This might not sound too exciting "today", but it sure was "yesterday"!

Parks have always been such an important element in helping to make cities complete. I remember Columbia Park, Olive Street Park, A.C. Steere Park the Fair Grounds Park, but the biggest and best has always been Betty-Virginia Park. A.C. Steere, a prominent local builder whose home still stands overlooking the park, had a daughter named Virginia. Across Trabue Street lived Mr. Goldstein whose daughter was named Betty – hence Betty-Virginia Park. I can't begin to imagine how many hundreds of thousands of children have had their lives enriched by pure fun in that park.

When I was 10 years old, I had my birthday party at Betty-Virginia Park. Having an April birthday was a perfect time as far as the weather was concerned. We parked the black Dodge on Ockley Drive and walked over the brick and concrete bridge which was the park's main entrance at that time. The pavilion was a perfect place for a party with its red tile roof, open sides, concrete tables and benches. What fun!

Everyone loved to go to Betty-Virginia because if had the biggest of everything – or so I thought! The see-saws were 12 feet long, the swings were 50 feet high, the rings were 30 feet tall, the monkey bars were 20 feet long, and the slide was 40 feet high. Fast forward to 2006 – for some reason the swings, slides, and all the other playground equipment seem to have SHRUNK! Honestly, I did not know that metal could do that!

Through the years since I was a child, I've enjoyed Betty-Virginia, through my own eyes, my daughters' eyes and my grandchildren's eyes. When you realize the park stretches from Line to Fairfield Avenues and from Ockley Drive to the Trabue hill, that's a pretty big park – was and still is.

Going to the park for recreation is a national pastime which I hope and pray will never end. There will always be a child living inside our bodies regardless of our present age. We cannot erase the memories of those hot summer days or cold winter days spent at Betty-Virginia or any of the other wonderful parks our city operates. What a blessing it is to enjoy the out-of-doors with good friends at parks which really are sacred ground.

At my age when I drive down Line or Fairfield, I slow down a little to see if I can hear some parent saying to their child as she pushes the swing –

> "How do you like to go up in a swing,
> Up in the air so blue?
> Oh, I do think it's the pleasantest thing
> Ever a child can do!"

4th of July Remembrances

The Fourth of July is coming. Just thought I'd warn you if you haven't read the newspaper ads. It's also our national birthday.

My patriotism probably stems from the fact that on Sunday, Dec. 7, 1941, the Japanese bombed Pearl Harbor. I was in the fourth grade, and my world history lessons had not included the location of that island.

However, I thought my life was going to end. We were at WAR! What did I know about war? The closest I could relate was playing cowboys and Indians.

When July Fourth appeared the next year, Shreveport went red, white and blue. We were not only aware of our present war, but all the wars our wonderful country had taken part in since July 4, 1776.

Americans were thankful for our leaders, our country and most of all, for the men and women who sacrificed their lives to protect and defend us.

With victory in war comes a variety of memorials. The most meaningful for me are the Tomb of the Unknown Soldier and Normandy Beach.

The Tomb sits high on a hill in Arlington Cemetery overlooking the Potomac River.

As I stood there I felt like that soldier and thousands of others he represented, standing at attention waiting for that final bugle call to charge.

Following is a tribute I wrote for friends when their son was killed in Iraq.

Their little boy was as good as gold
Always did what he was told.
He learned to mind the Golden Rule,
Loving life he was nobody's fool.
He studied hard and learned a lot,
Friends came easy, his life was hot.
The life he knew was proud and safe,
He wanted little, there was no waste.

But then the world turned upside down,
All hell broke loose at zero ground.
Life was a puzzle he couldn't solve,
Too many problems to be resolved.
He loved his country, God and creed,
Knew in his mind what America would need.
Loyal young men and women, too
Vowed to protect our red, white and blue.
He signed his name on the dotted line,
Told us all he'd be just fine.
"We must be free to put our trust
In a land we love when life is just."
He left our home with a brave new heart,
To prove the enemy could not make his mark.
On this our land of honor and law
With his eyes on the flag, that's what he saw.
He trained, he fought, he did his best,
It seemed to all he passed the test.
But war is hell and those who survive
Will tell the world, "It's a bloody ride."
Their boy died but not in their hearts,
He'll live every day and play the part
Of a hero to all who fought for right
To keep our freedom strong and bright.

CHRISTMAS PAST

Remember when Christmas was CHRISTMAS? If you are under 40 reading this and don't know what I'm referring to ask an OLD person – they can fill you in.

Mother didn't start Christmas shopping until Rubenstein's decided it was time. This might sound confusing so I'll explain and try to remember. The store on Milam had two entrances on either side of a middle display window, measuring 8 feet across and 12 feet deep. Behind this was the front door of the store. In this window was the biggest, sweetest-looking, most jovial, perfectly attired Santa Claus ever invented. As a little girl I'd stand with my nose pressed against the glass (adding my imprint to many others) and laugh every time he laughed. I'm almost positive he was mechanically rigged, but who cared, it was Santa Claus!

Each store had its own version of Christmas, but after Rubenstein's came Sears. On the toy floor you could find a real Santa Claus. The line was always long but the wait was worth it. Each child was eager to sit on his lap and have a "private" talk with him concerning choices of toys while parents strained to listen.

The Christmas morning I most remember was finding my electric train set. Daddy worked for the KCS so you can imagine my joy — except it didn't work. Daddy did everything he could to fix it but nothing worked. After Christmas holidays he bought me another one. Years later he explained that he bought the train on a business trip to Kansas City. He and the hotel night clerk played with my train so much they broke it! With no time to replace it — I got the broken one. (Both "boys" were in their forties)

Christmas of 1950 I was a Freshmen at Centenary and was quite impressed with myself having been invited to the KA Christmas formal at the beautiful Chrystal Ball Room. My date, a good-looking senior, picked me up in a new car – how cool was that?

Mother with her needle in hand had made me the most beautiful white, full-skirted, hooped formal with a sequined strapless top. Daddy said I looked beautiful and mother and I agreed.

At intermission the girls at our table excused ourselves and went to the powder room where we exchanged all sorts of tales. Finishing our visit we started walking across the dance floor when I heard someone say, "Look at JoJo!" Of course I acknowledged them with a smile but more people were laughing and pointing. I finally looked around to utter embarrassment! There was a 6 foot piece of toilet paper stuck to the net of my dress! No words are necessary here to explain my anguish. Thank goodness I recovered and due to my sense of humor I did not kill myself when I got home. Telling my parents the next day was bad enough. They laughed every time I went to a formal and made sure to advise me to check my skirt.

Kings Highway Christian Church always produced a Christmas pageant. Daddy was asked to be a wiseman and naturally he had the most lavish costume Mother could produce. As he came down the aisle with his gift we were so proud. As the wisemen knelt they removed their hats and a huge sound of snickering was heard. We all have visually pictured these men, but not one ever had as bald a head as my daddy! I loved it, as I do ALL bald headed men!

Christmas and Hanukkah come but once a year, and I wished it was like it used to be, but its not. I've had many different Christmases just as each of you have — just think back – as a child, young adult, bride/groom, wife/husband, mother/father, widow/widower, grandmother/father, and great-grandmother/father. Each level presents different circumstances from which we learn great lessons for living. Let us not forget family and friends who will have their first "heavenly" Christmas. Take time to reaffirm your individual beliefs of Christmas and Hanukkah. GOD BLESS US EVERY ONE!

CHILDHOOD AND WWII

Last Friday's column dealt with the blissful life of a girl growing up in the '30s and '40s. Our summers were honestly "the good, the bad and the beautiful". One poet reminds us "into each life some rain must fall".

Those rainy days began in 1941 and World War II. We traded many of our happy pastimes with serious ones and never regretted it for a moment for four summers.

Neighborhood friends took to their tasks bravely. We peeled the foil off of every piece of gum and off the inside packaging of cigarettes. The foil was wrapped into a ball, once reaching a circumference of 17 inches. I wondered what the diameter was (I had just learned about that.) Daddy explained it using "pi". Lost me on that. I like cherry pie, but that never entered the conversation.

We collected grease in big Snowdrift cans placed in my wagon. Each neighbor would heat their grease and pour it into our can. Grease was used in making glycerin for ammunition.

Spare rubber, metal, tin cans and anything that could be salvaged was collected. This truly is where recycling began.

All of these collectibles were sold at different locations. With our money we bought 10-cent "defense stamps" to be placed into a folder. Upon reaching $18.75, we put them aside to mature to $25. Victory gardens were very popular. If you had any land or a big flower bed, it was changed into a garden for food. Tomatoes, okra, onions and lots of other vegetables were traded among friends.

There were government stamps for meat, sugar, butter and cooking oil. Stamps were also necessary for gas, tires and shoes.

Our daily lives were devoted to the war effort and we discovered age made no difference. We were consumed with loyalty, service and dedication to peace. Tom Brokaw proclaimed this was the greatest generation. He neglected to include the entire citizenry on American soil. Everyone fought to win and was successful.

Another dark and rainy day brought infantile paralysis – polio. We were scared. A summertime disease made it easy for parents to confine their children. It took its toll on my friends. Patsy Laird and Flo Williams. No known source of carrier was ever discovered, but Dr. J. Salk discovered a vaccine.

After the war and polio, our city began to enjoy summers again – those wonderful three months away from school. It's hard to believe our summers could be defined as beautiful since we had no air conditioning. Our neighborhood surrounded the Shriners Hospital. Before the original building was demolished it was evident when the operating room on the second floor was being used.

Gathering on the steps of Dan's house, we children prayed the child up there would be able to run and walk, have a straight back, hold a spoon or hold his head up. What a wonderful deed Shriners provided for those in need.

Other beautiful days we ate watermelon on Greenwood Road, slept on porches, took family vacations, took the trolley to town to go to the library, the fabulous Strand Theatre and made new friends.

These were the good old days – days in our young lives about which we still reminisce – good, bad and beautiful.

COLLEGE HARD ON MOTHERS

Here we go again – School Time! As I've said, what's wrong with <u>after</u> Labor Day?

Fall of 1950, high school graduate, and I was on my way. After completing 12 grades I had visions of boarding the KCS and traveling to college – didn't happen! I was Shreveport bound! With a heavy heart, I took to my pen to express myself.

In 1950, I pondered my life ahead after Byrd where was I to be led? My friends were packing, excited to leave for colleges and universities you wouldn't believe!

My head held high, my future bright, I wondered which school would be just right. With their minds made up my Mom & Pop drove me to college – down 10 city blocks. I loved my Centenary, but something was missing yet I got my share of dating and kissing. Then autumn brought those football games and that's where I'd lost – no team to claim!

Centenary wasn't too bad because I made a lot of friends. Dorm curfews were 9:00 on Friday nights and 10:00 on Saturdays. I lived at home and mine was 11:00. I can still hear Daddy walking around the living and dining rooms counting sleeping bodies on the floor. "15", he said. "Count again, there's supposed to be 17," mother answered. He found the other 2 quickly. A huge breakfast was prepared, and each girl received a parental hug and kiss which were welcomed by homesick freshmen.

My point in relating my story is this. I swore if I had children they would attend college at least 200 miles away. I wanted them to have experiences of going away to college, football game parties, and talk about it forever. (I'm still mad at my parents when September rolls around!)

After Byrd, my first-born Anne chose the University of South Louisiana in Lafayette. She and her roommate Karen Adams organized their room, got classes scheduled and pledged a sorority. She was set for 4 years of college and I was thrilled.

Thrilled – good grief – I was a basket case. My 2 daughters and I are very close. She was there and I was here. Was she happy, were classes too hard, did people like her, did she have clean underwear, was she hungry? My God – what have I done?

Her phone calls were all positive, yet I worried. I discovered each morning when I awoke I could hardly swallow. Orvis said to see a doctor – so I went to 1-2-3. No one could diagnose my condition. Number 4 was Dr. Juan Watkins who asked, "Does it feel like a lump in your throat?" "Yes, yes, will I die before Anne comes home for Thanksgiving?" He explained that something in my throat swelled because of being upset. "Take this tiny tranquilizer in the morning, and you'll be cured." He saved my life!

I did something very resourceful to help my Empty Nest Syndrome even though I still had a precious little Liz bird nesting at the table each night. As I delivered her to _her_ first day of school Liz asked, "Mommy, are you sure I'm old enough for school?" I cried all day!

In AA the participants have a sponsor for help. I organized Mothers Anonymous! I promised to listen, cry, offer suggestions and even lunch. I still offer these services. (At my age I might start Wives of Retirees!)

Sharing these feelings about Anne's departure is still important to me and helpful to others. For 18 years children rely on us for _everything_ then no more, or so they think. Being a mother is tough, but being a college student's mother is the next chapter. I wasn't the first and far from the last.

Young mothers, get advice from _your_ mothers and _their_ mothers! We do survive, it's a miracle!

DRUGSTORES

Remember when we watched the schools' clocks waiting for the 3:00 bell? Maybe time isn't as important to me as in the past. I was told the older you get the less time you have. I've calculated and I'm down to about 18 hours compared to others who still have 24!

I guess I've moved on because I found myself driving down Line Avenue in the midst of school traffic. I glanced at the Glenwood sign – once again – my how times change.

My first memory of Glenwood Drugstore was sitting in our car waiting for the "Carhop". Why, in the summertime, would we do that when going inside made better sense? Because it was the 1930s.

Ice cream orders consisted of Banana Splits with 3 dips of ice cream, syrup of choice, whipped cream plus a cherry. An "Idiot's Delight", served in a huge brandy snifter, had multiple dips, scodes of extras, nuts and cherries. Meant to serve 4, it was a "Delight" after a day in non air-conditioned Byrd.

Booths seated 4 or more. The marble counter had revolving stools which provided the customer the opportunity of surveying the room for possible dating purposes.

The other side of the drugstore contained the usual store items. At the cosmetic counter were samples of perfume to try. Mother's favorite was Evening in Paris in a cobalt blue bottle. I can still smell it.

"Meet me at the drugstore," was heard in the halls from locker to locker. Once there we laughed, talked about boys, girls, grades, everything. It was a perfect hangout before and after the football games because they were played in the stadium on Gladstone. A perfect ending of a day in high school.

Walgreen's on the corner of Texas and McNeil was a destination sometimes on a weekend night. A vendor sold popcorn from a 2 wheel popper using long sacks and just wide enough to retrieve a fist full of wonderfully hot popcorn. Nothing like it!

After that treat we made our way up to Sear's Corner. All stores were open late on Saturdays for shoppers who couldn't get to town during the week. Gathered at the corner was the uniformed Salvation Army Band. Shoppers standing by would join in singing hymns and donate money to this very worthy organization which still provides services to our community today.

Ligget's Drugstore on Texas was quaint. I had my first club sandwich there – a Dagwood Bumstead creation. We sat in black wrought iron chairs at small tables before or after attending movies at the Don, Majestic, Capital or the Joy – our choice.

I talked to Jimmy Weyman, or Jimmy Weyman talked to me, about his Dad's Broadmoor Drugstore. Built in 1938 at Youree and Ockley it housed pharmacists, regular drugstore merchandise of that day and a long marble soda fountain with stools, booths and a juke box.

At 14 Jimmy was a soda jerk preparing all the fountain orders which were shouted to him by the carhops. Shoot a pair mean 2 cokes; choc-dust, malt; choc on, sundae. If Jimmy answered with "86" it meant "we're out of it".

On weekends and nights the parking lot was full with carhops hopping from car to car. Pay was $9 weekly with free food and drinks. But what a way to learn to remember orders, make change and be "good will ambassadors of Broadmoor Drugs."

Drugstores were popular meeting places for teens and adults. Many of our future Civic leaders, doctors, business executives and lawyers worked there. It was good to be seen there with your date after a show or the dance.

Everyone had a favorite drugstore – Williams on Southern, Weyman on Fairfield, Corner Drug on 70th. Wouldn't you like to drive up, let the window down, honk and order "shoot-a-pair" to Ed Jones?

FATHERS AND INFLUENCE

"A rose by any other name would smell as sweet," to quote Shakespeare. He unknowingly originated the idea that a man who fathers a child could be labeled a multitude of names. In my family alone, there's Daddy, Dad, Dadee, Pop, Pap and Grandad. Now we have great grandchildren. No telling what the name might be when they learn to talk. They might be so totally confused that they will call us by our given names, which would really be a lot simpler.

"Father names" have no bearing on how big, how small, red headed, grey, bald or anything your father is – he's yours!

Fathers and mothers have such an influence on our being in every area of our existence. However, there is a difference which is not intentional, not obvious or contrived – it's just human nature.

I asked Judy Moore how her father Jimmy Patterson had influenced her. She is blessed with his love of England, theatre, books, and a wonderful sense of humor. She referred to him as a Renaissance Man. He also played college football and loved other sports.

Mildred Lee and Lila Mills' father was Dr. Mastin Scott, a general practitioner in the 30's and 40's. They didn't see him too often because of office hours, hospital rounds, and house calls. He must have passed on a love of caring and compassion because his daughters exhibit these qualities with friends and in the teaching professions. It's amazing how those genes keep on moving around. 60 years after Dr. Scott's death he is still remembered for his medical knowledge and kindness to his patients.

Ralph Brandon's daughter Ann was my next source of information. I asked her to describe her late father and I quote, "Daddy was adamant about education, a gift he'd never realized beyond high school. He took education a step further: learning about people and customs. He commanded my exposure to different cultures and situations. I have traveled extensively across America, meeting her people and learning her ways and have benefited from my friendships during these interesting and educational sojourns. I attribute that wonderful itch called 'wanderlust' to Daddy's encouragement and credit his guidance for so many wonderful life experiences."

My daughters Anne and Liz lost their father at early ages. We were devastated, but I was more concerned that they would grow up without the benefit of a father, which in my heart would be hell on earth. I had played the "2 parent" role for 2 ½ years when "we met and married Orvis." For 37 years he has filled the Daddy shoes night and day, year after year, wedding after wedding, grandchild after grandchild, happy times and sad times. You just can't get any better than that.

I believe all fathers want boy babies and mine was no exception. I was named Joanne, but he called me Jo until I married. He did everything possible to teach me all he would have taught a boy. By 8 I had learned to saw and use the hammer, always remembering to spit on the nail's point which allowed it to slide into the wood easier. I used the leveler with the bubble, the "L" square, and the rule of cleaning up your mess. Come to think of it, Mother was trying to teach me the same thing in my room!

I was a spoiled rotten brat with nice manners. I probably still am, but I try to hide it. I did not get this way alone – I had to be trained and Daddy was successful.

I lived at home until I married. We did that back then. Every Sunday morning Daddy got in my bed and read the Funny Papers to me. He knew darn well I was 25 years old and had a B.A. in English! Good habits are hard to break.

One more piece of knowledge was brought to my attention by Daddy. He told me that when I saw birds sitting on electric lines, they are having school or on Sunday it's church. They are learning how to sing, fly, find worms, and dive for bugs. Look up and watch them, you might learn something.

And then there are substitutes for fathers; step-fathers, grandfathers, uncles, neighbors, teachers – the list goes on. These men have stepped up to the plate and filled a most difficult role. Each man and child must give and take because they weren't born together. It is a matter of choice, and that's what life is. Sometimes it takes and sometimes it doesn't.
During WWII, Daddy filled in for the three Boutee' boys when their Daddy was fighting in Europe for 2 years. What a void these children had to endure.

Before Orvis, my Daddy filled the role for my daughters. They adored him. In a letter to him in the nursing home, Liz wrote, "Thank you for giving me things to talk about, "When I was little my Granddaddy and I….!"

Sunday, June 17th, I hope you take a few minutes to say from your heart how very much you love him, admire him, and how special it is to have him as your Father/Daddy. It might be nice to tell him more than once a year!

I've discussed all sorts of men with different admirable qualities. Put them all together and you'll have the perfect FATHER, but I'd rather have my Daddy any time. Wouldn't you?

P.S. Don't forget the one person who made it possible that your Dad is your Dad! Love thy mothers, too!

FUN DOWNTOWN

Remember when we went TO town, DOWN town, or UP town, depending on where you lived? Shreveport had one major shopping area which included Texas, Milam, McNeil, and Marshall Streets. As a native I am ashamed I don't know more street names, but I could tell you where each store was in relation to another store or the Court House.

Shopping in the dark ages was a terrific experience. We either went by car or trolley. Serious shopping to town meant one could buy a car, fur coat, garden hose, a pair of hose with or without seams, hats, or washing machine just by walking a few blocks. Talk about one stop shopping! If you shopped all Saturday you might see your neighbor in 4 or 5 different stores.

During the school year entertainment was limited to football games, and then originality raised its head. Mary Clare, Banny, Betsy, and I would catch the trolley and be in town by 10:00. Dime stores were a fun destination with candy counters where I was initiated to maltballs, red hots, candy corn, chocolate covered cherries, you name it. All were sold by the pound which made it possible to buy anything and any number. Sweet tooth? No, Sweet teeth!

Several Dime stores had luncheon counters, one of which had the best hot open-faced beef sandwich! We've recently met Tom who as a young man was the manager of one of those counters. He has sweet memories of serving customers a vast choice of foods and drinks.

And while you were eating, there was a music counter where a pianist would play sheet music for you before purchasing it. That was a classy Dimestore!

Finishing our tour of Texas Street we would end up at Sue Peyton's Dress Shop housed on the second floor above Ligget's Drugstore. She was Mary Clare's mother, and I'm sure she shuttered when she heard us climbing the stairs. We tried on clothes and watched as young brides modeled their dresses until she suggested we leave Texas street and visit Milam Street stores!

Texas had a wonderful variety of stores where "anything" could be purchased. C.C. Hardman Paint, Don Cohen Shoes, Wiseman's toys were all in the first block. My Storybook dolls came from Wisemans which I still have. Made of porcelain with beautiful hair, the 4 in dolls only made it into my girls' hands when the thermometer reached 102° and they were confined to bed!

Next block was Sears, buy anything. Peggy and I even took tap dancing there one summer. Bakers, Lipscomb's, then Hearnes, where we chose our china and crystal, Jean's Hosery, & Levy's with its ancient ticket delivery system exposed on the ceiling as it was sent upstairs to the office, and Phelps where they had an X-ray box to see where your toes were in the shoes!

Across the street were Penney's, Jordan & Booth, Peacocks, & O.P.O. & Milam Street was host to Goldrings, Selbers, Harris' Newstadts, and Rubensteins. On side streets were Flournoy/Harris where engagement and wedding rings and anything silver was sold. On McNeil was Palais Royal, my favorite the Fashion, and Dryers.

The most wonderful and outstanding quality of these stores was the fact that the owners were "on the floor" all the time, overseeing employees, stock, and most of all happy customers. They were hosts and you were their guests – feeling very special!

By noon we had stacked up hours of female adventures. Lunch time was on its way to meet us at Morrison's or Big Chain Cafeterias, Baptist Tea Room (best yeast rolls in <u>America</u>, Columbia and Dehan's Restaurants or the Dimestores. Meals depended on how much money you could talk your mother out of. Finishing lunch we were off to the Picture Shows at the Strand, Don, Majestic, Capitol, and Joy plus pop corn & candy.

Having all day to enjoy, we could not have been happier teenagers as we boarded our respective trolleys bound for home. We knew we were lucky to have clothes, trolleys, friends, parents, and friends. After viewing all the horrible 1941-45 newsreels, we realized how fortunate we were – we survived "the War".

GRADE SCHOOL

Remember when going to grade school was so simple. It was the high point of your Monday thru Friday. Mine started at the breakfast table with my family. I quickly brushed my teeth, dressed and said goodbye.

My Alma Mater is Barret. The last time I visited was a zillion years ago, but on my way down Fairfield I always glance at Barret Place. Mr. Thomas Barret built his home in 19___ and sold pieces of land as the city progressed. Eventually the school board built a school which honored him.

Grade school consisted of seven grades. My teachers (so I thought) were sweet little old ladies who loved everyone except one or two boys, who were "straightened out" by the end of the first six weeks.

My favorite teachers were Annie Merril Scarborough and Mildred Chance. They are responsible for my choosing to be a teacher. My other five teachers were also outstanding because they taught us where our parents left off.

The grading system was quite unique. You either made an "S" for satisfactory or "U" for unsatisfactory, or heaven forbid an "S"! My parents were rather disappointed when I arrived at Byrd and made an assortment of A's, B's, & C's.

Math was also interesting. Miss Bartoff insisted we borrow differently from the acceptable way in subtraction. Test your friends, Barret Alumni.

My first experience in reading was about Dick and Jane. I hated those little kids! All they did was played with Spot, jump, skip, and jump. Why didn't "they" make up their beds, go to school, or wash dishes?

Last week I decided to visit Barret Street Grade School. My heart jumped up into my throat as if I was entering for the first time. My heart jumped up into my throat as if I was entering for the first time. The front porch and steps on which we played seemed much shorter and narrower than I remembered. As I entered the hall the principal's office was on the left.

Miss Bartoff was a severe disciplinarian – you didn't cross her. Just looking at her was a chore because she was about 100 years old! One day she winked at me or it could have been something in her eye. About that time I learned that we had the same name! I had it made.

Her curriculum was perfect. Those dedicated teachers went over and beyond their duties. Madeline Rogers, second grade teacher taught us about safety in the home, especially fires. She took the class on a walking trip to the fire station on the corner of Line Avenue and Wilkinson. On the way back someone asked if we could build a fire station. With the help of some 7th grade boys we did build a two story fire station complete with a "pole" in the corner of her room.

Julia Rogers was my 4th grade teacher when WWII started in December. We were studying World Georgraphy so she took this opportunity to educate us about all the theatres of war. Our Weekly Readers also informed us of Generals, Admirals, names of ships, and types of planes. We were Americans big or little. The newsreels at the picture shows completed our education about war.

Stunt night in the Municipal Auditorium was a competition among all Caddo Parish grade schools. Each provided a 15 minute program. Barret won with a beautiful production of Tchaikovsky's "Waltz of the Flowers". Each child was completely re-born as a flower, bird, or bug. I was a red butterfly who flew on my tiptoes from flower to flower. Moments like these are hard to forget – I fell!

Janet Lucas was the director of the choral club for 5th, 6th, and 7th graders. We sang opera, broadway show tunes, Ave Maria in Latin and loved every note.

My visit to Barret was a success. My town director took me to the auditorium, cafeteria, down the halls with the rooms full of memories, and the playground.

The principal was very friendly and graciously welcomed me as did her office staff and teachers. The school was neat as could be, the students were well-behaved and full of energy.

Thank you Barret for such a grand visit – you made S+!

GRADUATION

School's out! Let's go to the next level . . whatever that may be. Those of us who have graduated, let's lend a helping hand to 2007's class. Here's my story.

I've really enjoyed reading the articles concerning the graduations of the high schools and colleges in our area. There were pictures of honor students, whose GPA was probably higher than mine, speakers and locations for the ceremonies. Of course, I'm always a little upset by the dates, but no one asked me. I started school after Labor Day and got out the last week of May. I just wish we had had the luxury of air conditioning! I might have made better grades!

As I absorbed all of this knowledge I began to reflect on my own graduation. I consulted Webster's and he said; #1 to grant an academic degree or diploma, #2 to pass from one step of experience, proficiency or prestige to a higher one.

I was proud to know that I had qualified for number 1, and on several occasions I qualified for number 2.

My first graduation was from C.E. Byrd High School in 1950. The female graduates were dressed in long white dresses and carried a dozen red roses. The young men wore suits, white shirts and ties. We walked down the Gladstone sidewalk from the school to the football field, which was washed in bright lights. The graduates sat in chairs on risers and faced the stadium, which now has been demolished. There were mothers, fathers, siblings, grandparents, and many more who were interested or connected with this memorable night. Graduation is definitely a family thing. This night was one to be remembered and talked about for years to come. Since there were only two public high schools in Shreveport at that time, I'm sure 80% of the audience had made this same walk to the next step in their lives. Talk about tradition . . .

My next graduation was from Centenary College, and once again it was held outside in the amphitheatre. I finally had my chance to wear that cap and gown, and most of all that moment when I moved the tassel from one side of my mortar board to the other – a very significant act.

Wow – here I am, a college graduate! I was 22 years old, and had completed 16 years of school plus kindergarten. I had been taught to add 2 + 2, to read about Bob and Nancy, geometry (who needs that?), and how to be a teacher! (That is not taught, it's "on the job training").

In 1955 a friend and I were counselors at a summer camp. We lived in cabins with wood-burning fireplaces. As I bedded down that first night, I noticed there was an inscription on the mantle, which read "the journey of a thousand miles begins with the first step".

With a college degree and one year of teaching behind me, I felt rather accomplished in the first 23 years of my life. Was I in for a big surprise! Looking back, I realize I had only taken baby steps.

At the 50th reunions of both high school and college, graduation memories were still being talked about – first the weather, about 85 degrees the last week of May does make an impression. Next topic – what are you going to do now? Help! Which college? What job? Talk about a thousand mile journey! I didn't feel like putting on my shoes much less going on a journey! However, by now, it's 2007 and I think I've probably been 100 times a thousand miles, but so have all my friends.

As I wrote several years ago:

>Through the years we've laughed and cried
>Somehow gracefully we learned to survive.
>We're married, divorced, been widowed, and remarried
>Survived parenthood and the burdens we carried.
>In the past fifty years which seem so short
>We've approached our peak with grateful hearts.
>Life goes on with all sorts of stories,
>We laugh and cry but try not to worry . . .

As for graduation's definition, I'll add #3, struggle to survive and learn from it. #2 is a total mixture of hundreds of emotions and experiences. If you say you weren't affected by graduation, you aren't being honest with yourself.

Personally – I wouldn't have missed graduating for a zillion dollars because it still happens every day of my life in some mysterious way. Aren't we lucky to be that "graduate"?

GRANDPARENTS

Remember when….

….you went to your grandparent's house? Mine died, when I was young. I have enjoyed seeing my children with my parents. The bond between them is so full of sweet memories. Hopefully, I can learn by example to "grandmother" perfectly. The following is a letter written by Liz, my daughter. Through her words one can understand that special relationship between my parents and their grandchildren.

Dear Mamma and Daddie,

I sure do miss seeing you both since you went to the nursing home. I hope you never forget how much I love you and how much you mean to me. I will never forget the two of you and all the memories we have shared. You are the best grandparents a girl could ever have.

Thank you for being so good to me. Thank you for the peanut butter sandwiches you made when you took Anne and me to Texarkana on the KCS Railroad. Thank you for letting me drive Daddie's truck, endless times up and down the driveway when I was just 6 years old. We waved to you, Mamma, every time we passed the kitchen window, surely we drove you crazy. Thank you for buying malted milk balls at Sears. Thank you for going in halves with me when I didn't have enough money to buy something I "needed". Thank you for making good hamburgers and spaghettios and for not telling Mom when we were bad. Thank you for talking to me about the Depression and helping me to open my eyes to the past – I made an A+ on my interview. Thank you for making the cross stitch sampler I sewed to come true. "If Mother says no – ask Grandmother. If all else fails, ask Grandfather." Thank you for teaching me the true meaning of being a good grandparent. Thank you for giving me things to talk about, "When I was little my Grandparents and I used to..". Thank you Daddie for teaching me how to be carsick by constantly pumping the gas pedal. Thank you for teaching me how to make the best toast with strawberry preserves. Thank you for waking me up in the middle of the night to go to the bathroom! Thank you for taking the place of my own Daddy for 2 ½ years. Thank you for all the gum….and cavities! Thank you for teaching me how to cane pole fish. Thank you for pinching me on my bottom and making that funny noise. Thank you for letting me put shaving cream on my face and shave with an empty razor while you were really shaving. Thank you for letting me ride on your back, for swinging me higher than any girl has ever swung before. Thank you for all the times I sat on your lap and be loved. Thank you for building our playhouse, for giving me presents, too, when it was Anne's birthday. Thank you for letting us spend the night at your house, for teaching me to like the Lawrence Welk Show. Thank you for telling me sooooo many times the stories of *The Three Bears* and *Red Riding Hood and the Big Bad Wolf*. Thank you for building my bug box out of the Hush Puppy shoe box, which I still have. Thank you for picking those berries so we could have all those cobblers. Thank you for raising your daughter right so she could, in turn, raise her daughters, me and Anne, to be good little girls and proper ladies. Thank you for always looking so nice when you left your house. Thank you for being loved by so many people. Thank you for saying, "You'll never know how much I love you," "I love you more than anyone else, you are my favorite," which I am sure you told all your grandchildren! Let me just say those things all back to you because I <u>do</u> love you more than anyone else, you <u>are</u> my favorite and I <u>do</u> know how much you love me! I'll never forget those wet kisses, too.

    I'd better go because I'm running out of tears. I love you both so much, my darlings. Your favorite, Liz. Happy Grandparents Day!

HALLOWEEN

Remember when Halloween was so simple? Decorations adorned the stores only two weeks prior to the Spooky Day.

As I remember Mother saved an old sheet for me to dress as a ghost -- what else! Don't forget we were growing up in the "pre and war years", our sheets were probably older than the war! I did get a new mask every year which probably cost 25¢. I don't remember who the masks represented, but they were scary. I convinced myself I was non-recognizable except what ghost had long black curls! We carried orange pumpkins made of paper mache' and tried our best to be the first one to fill it with goodies.

Trick or Treat meant exactly that – if the homeowner doesn't give you a "treat", you'll give him/her a trick. Somehow it never got <u>that</u> far.

We were warned by our parents to be careful crossing streets – <u>that</u> was the most horrendous act standing in our way of an exciting night.

If you were fortunate in having brave and completely fun-loving parents you hosted a party. The most fun game for me was bobbing for apples in a wash tub half full of water. You couldn't use your hands, just your nose to push the apple next to the side and then your teeth to take a huge bite and bring it out of the water. I liked apples before and after this challenge.

Frances used to blindfold her guests at her parties and describe to the unsuspecting what they were feeling: Brains (spaghetti) and eyes (grapes). The object was to identify what body part they were feeling – in my neighborhood we called it "Operation." Funny that none of them were led to the medical profession!

My favorite Halloween party was with my new friends in the eighth grade from Broadmoor. It was at Janie's house for boys and girls. We played a few card games and Bingo then got down to the real stuff – "Spin the Bottle". I don't remember the rules but when that 5¢ coke bottle was spun and pointed to me the cutest boy I'd ever seen took me to the Dining Room and kissed me – in the mouth no less! My goodness, I had been kissed by a total stranger! During the rest of the game and there after I made sure I knew <u>who</u> I was kissing!

Betty always played spooky music for her children and neighbors, Glenn Ellen rang the doorbells and ran, Patsy and her friends tricked and treated Baltimore Street, Jean and Pat, and the rest of us remembered having hot dogs and hot chocolate.

Carolyn and her friends got up nerve to visit Barret Place on Fairfield where they were welcomed with cokes and cookies by the Barrets.

In my Broadmoor neighborhood, I've always dressed up for the children because I wanted them to realize it wasn't just another day for stores to make money. I scared the minister's little girl one year that she didn't speak to me until Easter.

Orvis and I babysat for our grandchildren one year and I was determined I would make it memorable. At 9 and 7 they were old enough to scare someone else and have fun doing it. Each wore a huge orange trash bag tied around the neck, a witch's mask and pointed black hat. Sitting still on either side of the walk they were told to jump up as the visiting children reached for a treat! It was a tremendous success because the minister, etc. had moved and our neighbors knew to expect the unexpected from ME!

October 31, "All Hallow's Eve," is the eve of All Saints Day, a Christian feast in honor of all saints. My Episcopal prayer book asks our maker "to help us to persevere in running the race that is set before us...until we attain eternal joy." As Winston Churchill said, "Never give up, never".

HANGOUTS

Remember when….

....I wrote about Drugstores a couple of weeks ago? It aroused a lot of sleeping memories. Not that we're old, it's that over the past 80 years we've had so much information stored in our memory banks it's difficult to bring the good stuff front and center. We sympathize and tend to finish each others sentences. Thank goodness we have a sense of humor or it could be embarrassing.

Our next door neighbor, Weezie, was 12 years older than I. She was my idol. When she got to Byrd I was allowed to ride in her car. After 3:00 she and her friends would take me to their favorite hang-out, "A Pig and a Whistle" on the Greenwood Road. For some unspeakable reason she had a crush on a Fair Park boy! Her friends supported her but it was not publicized! He was a cute carhop who gave her free chocolate shakes. I'd have driven up and honked, too.

Weber's Root Beer Drive-In was located at the corner of King's Highway and Alexander. Its name stated half the menu – Root Beer and food. Big glass mugs kept on ice were almost too cold to handle. I can still taste the icy root beer traveling down my throat by gravity. Of course you might end up with a headache, but it was worth it.

Buster's on Market Street across from Caddo Coffee was the most popular hang-out with a huge parking lot. Their carhops probably wore out more than one pair of shoes a school year. (This was before you wore tennis shoes for anything else but P.E.) Tips were meager because a hamburger cost 35¢ and coke was 10¢ times 2. With today's tipping standards he might get 15¢. That could buy you a coke next time. We had to think ahead in those days.

The best Bossier City drive-in was Amber Inn. No one went in but the joke was "amber in and stagger out". I ate my first shrimp burger there – what a treat!

There were two hang-outs on Kings Highway. "College-In" next to Broadmoor Garage was popular after school for students who had cars. I can still see girls wearing football jackets sitting in cars and inside. This must be where the "Happy Days" writer got his material. Just think what we could have done with cell phones!

The "Key Club", next to Murrell's, was started by a group of parents who wanted to provide a nice place for their teenagers to go. Members had a key for the front door, and were expected to be properly dressed with a date. There was a juke box, soft drinks and chaperones. Party manners were expected.

But – the best after school hang-out was Darrell's Grill across from the Glenwood. Katy and John of Eartheral Restaurante are probably still finding lost items from Byrd. Darrell's was owned by Pooley George's dad and served the best hamburgers, hot dogs, malts, shakes and fun times imaginable. It was also filled with cigarette smoke. I was accused of smoking by my parents – of which I was NOT guilty – until Centenary College and found the Cub, but that's another story. Darrell's was a before school, during school (if you were skipping), after school, after a game and open 6 days a week grill. Mr. George probably never got out of bed on Sundays.

It sounds like we ate hamburgers, etc. all the time – so what's new? We did get healthy food at home. A friend didn't like her dinner one night and her mother reminded her of the "starving children in Europe". "Send it to them," she responded. Worst spanking she ever got.

Personally, I don't know what young people do on dates now, but I'm convinced we had more fun. Hope I've cleaned a few cobwebs out of your memory banks and brought back your fun times.

HOME AND HEART

REMEMBER WHEN…

…You told someone "I want to go home" the first time? You meant business and those around you knew it and were hoping you'd get your request as soon as possible.

This time of year a lot of HOUSE/HOME sales appear. It's a chore requiring inner strength from all concerned. I've been fortunate because those who had me or married me were happy in Shreveport.

Thanks to Celia Smiley…"go to the dictionary." HOUSE: building which serves as living quarters for 1 or more families. HOME: social unit formed by a family living together.

After my college graduation friends found jobs, or to my Dad's disappointment, got married, not me! I wanted to see what was on the other side of the front door!

I landed a position with Longview High School teaching English and Speech, but where was I to live? A rented "room with kitchen privileges" became available. Later 2 teachers and I rented an apartment. For some reason I never referred to either as "HOME". The feeling was never there.

After teaching for several years I found that husband my parents had prayed for. During 10 ½ years in lived in a garage apartment, duplex, house and finally built in the country. I loved everything! It was close to my husband's business; my girls rode horses, had lots of company and acquired 2 dogs. That lasted about a week.
HELP, I'm HOMELESS! I was raised in town. I had no neighbors, lots of dirt, served coffee and lunch to farmer friends, and I was 7 MILES from a grocery store.

I called my parents trying not to whimper. "It's rather quiet down here. I don't think God knows where I live now." Mother, being her Edith Bunker-self reassured me, "I'll tell him tonight and give him your address." Prayer worked because I felt a sense of calm the next day because – I was at HOME.

4 years later my husband, Ben, died, and we 3 moved to town. The process began again producing a nice HOUSE, and we successfully turned it into a HOME.

After 3 years, we met another family who wanted to form a "social unit" with us. We searched and decided on a "building" for Orvis, Sally, Steve, Liz, Anne and me. It took a while for this new family to bond, but we were proud of our HOUSE becoming a HOME.

Several years later, my parents moved to the nursing home. The day I was to sign the papers I returned to 3020 and walked through each room yearning to hear the happy, funny and even sad words those walls had absorbed. Signing that sale was an act of betrayal – yet another link broken between parents and child.

Years later I discovered that my HOUSE had been sold again. Bursting into tears, the neighbor who comforted me said that it had been moved. How could this happen? That was my HOUSE, my HOME! I looked down and found a broken glass door knob. I brought it home just to remember. As Betty described her HOME, "a safe haven, full of memories, security and family."

Everyone has a special definition of HOME and HOUSE, no matter where or how you live. A room with kitchen privileges, apartment, a big, little, white, colored, wood or brick house or whatever makes you happy.

HOME is a word like love or friendship. You can't see, feel or really explain it, can't touch, buy or sell it. It's in your heart – the look in your eye as you drive in, when you talk about it and, most of all, when that front door opens. Then it's the people, the smells, the pets, "my chair" or a broken glass door knob that can make you feel good all over again.

It's 2007 and our social unit is 2 living at 474 for 37 years. We're happy.

Following church, the grocery store or a movie, one of us will say, "Let's go home." Those words are calming – they represent a sense of a day's accomplishment, renewal in a sheltered environment and rewarding in a zillion ways.

As Scarlett told Rhett, "Take me to Tara, take me HOME!"

HONORING VETERANS

Remember when we were in school collecting "everything for the WAR effort" and praying that our soldiers would survive and come home? The brave souls who fought in the Spanish-American, World Wars I and II, Korea, Vietnam, Desert Storm, and this war have to be the best and bravest Americans ever. November 11 is Veterans Day which honors them ALL.

Friends often recall where they were, how they felt and what the future would bring when President Roosevelt announced to the world that America was in a state of war. It affected every person differently. When I married Orvis who is now 85, he related his war history as a navy dive-bomber pilot flying off the U.S.S. Bennington Aircraft Carrier in the Pacific. Inscribed on his document of 3 Air Medals is this; "His courage and devotion to duty were in keeping with the highest traditions of the United States Naval Service, July 24,28, 1945." That's bravery for a 23 year old flying, bombing, sleeping, and eating when possible, and above all could feel his family's presence and progress, for his return.

Our neighbors, the Bouthe's, with 3 little boys were fatherless for 2½ years. No leave, no therapy, no calls, just letters once in a while --- that's how we at home survived for the duration of each war. Andre was a foot soldier meaning he fought on the ground, and honestly they won the war in Europe.

My friend Robbie served in Korea but never spoke of what he did. He returned with 2 frostbitten feet and eventually had both legs removed as a result. Robbie called and asked me to visit him in the hospital. When I arrived he wanted a "favor." "Of course," I said, "Anything for you!" "Joanne, would you be one of my pallbearers?" Dear God, what had I agreed to? For a friend that's the highest form of honoring that relationship.

Vietnam was also horrible. My "step-Sally's" husband flew bombing missions. With hundreds of POW's and MIA's bracelets with their names on them were distributed to citizens to be worn and prayed for. My Liz still prays for Peter Ganci and Thomas Mc Guiness. After finding their names on the wall in Washington war became very real.

I had the honor of sitting next to a distinguished Black man in my doctor's office. With a ready smile he greeted patients as they entered. We talked and told me "I'm 84 because I've lived a clean and good life because I believe in God and thank him everyday for protecting me in the war and bringing me home. 1943 til' 1945 I served in Okinawa, New Zealand, jungles if New Guinea with no food for 5 days and believed I'd never see America again? FORGET? NEVER!

The son of friends was killed in Iraq. Here's my tribute – An American Patriot.

LIFETIME FRIENDSHIPS

I like to test Webster's on words just to see who's smarter, or in a few cases, who's not so smart.

Friend: a) One attached to another by esteem or affection; b) Shows kindly interest and goodwill.

As far back as I can remember my first best friend was Kiki. Kiki came to work for my family two months before I was born. She was 17 and had never worked for a white family. This was during the Depression. When Kiki walked into our house she became one of us for 6 ½ days a week for almost 30 years. Kiki and I loved each other until she passed away.

She was my first confidant, adviser, secret keeper, protector from discipline ("nobody gonna switch my baby"), teacher, nurse and playmate. I had a good lesson of what a friend should be. Friends come in many categories, so I'll review a few of mine.

It was brought to my attention recently that a lot of my present friends are my high school friends. When you consider how small Shreveport was in the '40s and '50s, choice was limited. Our only sources were neighbors, schools and churches.

I was amused after I was admonished by my friend when I noticed how many high school reunions there are this year. Guess I'm in the majority there.

Family friends are sort of puzzling. As for the friend definition mentioned earlier, those qualities can be totally forgotten. But family – you've got them forever and ever. I couldn't resist looking up family in Webster's: A group of persons of common ancestry.

How's that for indentured. As of this day I am in a great friendship mode with my family – but that could change at any moment. Speaking of family friends leads me to my daughters.

There was something that rubbed me the wrong way about being friends with them when they were teenagers. I wanted to play the mother/daughter game – me the boss and they were the subjects. It just worked out best for us.

Honestly, I can admit that today at 49 and 47 they are best friends and my closest friends – thanks to time, experiences of being mothers, love and respect.

One of the best friends a woman can have is her OB/GYN. He can be lenient in pounds gained, travel and mood swings. Dr. Robert Wilson filled that spot in my life for 35 years listening to all my problems and complaints associated with being pregnant. He deserved a medal!

I attended Robert's funeral recently and was impressed with a point stressed by the minister. He examined the front of the program which stated Robert's birth and his death. Between these dates was a long "dash". He asked each attendee to reflect on what that dash meant to them. My 35 years brought back smiles and tears to me, especially with my daughter sitting next to me. Just think – he was the first human she saw when she was born. How can you have a better friend that that?

A wonderful high school friend calls often from Houston. These calls mean so much because it's great to realize that a male classmate has as much affection for the good old days as I do. We're talking about 65 years of friendships and we yearn to hear the news – good or bad – about those who became a part of our growing up.

My friend asked me if I remembered playing pick-up-sticks. He asked me to visualize the stacks of sticks after they were released. If you put a name on each stick just imagine how many contacts it makes with all of the other sticks. Just one touches 20 and those 20 touch 20 and so on.

The point is we have a relationship and influence with those we know and love and many we haven't even met yet. We are not alone, but surrounded by compassion, helpfulness and admiration. Isn't life grand when you have friends?

"When other friendships have been forgot – ours will still be hot."

LITTLE THEATRE

Remember When…

….going to see live theatre was unbelievable? Our only contact with characters telling stories was our parents and the picture show. I guess it was the dark ages, but look around us now.

After reading the reports in local newspapers, I am very impressed with our theatre achievements. Someone returning to Shreveport after a five year hiatus could not possibly have predicted our progress. Circumstances have blessed us with this golden opportunity to achieve success which can be profitable for all.

Our native sons, Bill Joyce and Bill Robison, are to be commended for their ventures. Their support systems are hard-working artists themselves. Behind every chief is a group of men, women, young and old, who, compensated or not, are working toward a common goal.

The acting business is not new. Comedy started with Aristophanes 345 B.C., the first writer of comedies. As far as I'm concerned it had its real beginning with William Shakespeare. As an old English/ Speech Major, I love his words after having to memorize soliloquies by well-known characters. If English teachers don't introduce students to him they'll never get it.

In 1945 Mary Clare's godmother, Mamie, decided we should be introduced to the finer things of life. Mamie insisted we buy season tickets to the Little Theatre. To verify our attendance she drove her 4 door black Chevy to pick us up and return us after every performance. These Plays were directed by John Wray Young and his wife, Margaret Mary. High school girls acted as ushers and snuffed the candles in the candelabras. The House was darkened and the curtain went up on great Plays.

My favorite production was the Barretts of Wimpole Street, the love story of Elizabeth Barrett and Robert Browning. When Elizabeth recited her sonnet, "How do I love thee, let me count the ways," I almost cried. Two weeks later I saw Elizabeth (Kay Brash Jeter who portrayed the role) in Big Chain grocery store. How is this possible? I finally mustered up nerve to compliment her performance.

She seemed very appreciative of me AND my age. Over the years I've recognized her and remembered my first theatre experience – a great beginning.

Betty Blanchard returned to Shreveport in the 40s and opened Courtyard Players, a theatre in the round. Considering the "stage area" was about 20 square feet, there were seats on each side totaling less than 200. Being so close to the performers was very intimate, drawing the audience and actors together as one. I'll never forget the "Glass Menagerie" then or recently when Patric McWilliams and Bob Buseick brought the play to Shreveport via his River City Reparatory Theatre. One more time to experience the oneness of theatre in the round.

Joe Gifford brought drama and comedy to us in the little white building at Centenary, the Playhouse, seating only 250. When he staged a play those seats were filled for every performance.

The Centenary Drama Festival held in 1954 was extraordinary. Three plays, "Romeo and Juliet", "Hamlet", and "Elizabeth the Queen", were staged on a bare stage with appropriate and minimal sets relating to each play. Actors in the principal rolls remained dedicated to those roles while supporting and minor roles rotated between three plays. According to "College Theatre" this was the premier of this type of staging.

The plays ran alternately each week – Hamlet – Mondays and Thursdays, etc. The run was 3 weeks. One might see the same audience 3 nights in a row – a little confusing but we had great reviews.

I don't know how Joe Gifford kept the scripts separated. Being stage manager I realized he was a genius. There was death in the last scene of each play. We stood shoulder to shoulder just inside the wings with eyes overflowing with tears – as did the audience. Now that's good theatre!

Local plays were so varied – comedy, tragedy or straight. Shreveporters could fill any role. Actors respected each director who had his own style and was never compared to the others.

The 30s, 40s and 50s created many enjoyable theatre experiences. All actors were volunteers (I looked it up): A person who expresses a willingness to undertake a service. No compensation – what a service! Just look at Shreveport today – House lights out – curtain up!

<u>Break a Leg</u>

MOTHER KEPT ME STYLISH

Remember those adages our parents used in teaching us how to be and not to be? One used on me until she died was "pretty is as pretty does". As I recall some of her pretty included what I wore – after all, "clothes do make the woman inside and out."

Mother loved to sew and make her own clothes while attending Shreveport High. Her Gusher picture shows her in a dark skirt and white middy blouse – the style of the day. I have several little baby apron dresses she made for me. The tiny stitches would rival any Singer!

In the Dark Ages, girls only wore dresses to school and Mother made mine. The wonderful experience of going to town to shop for fabric was indescribable. Hearne's, Sears, Rubenstein's and Penney's had bolts of material for every occasion. It was an opportunity to shop, choose, feel the fabric, look for buttons, thread and, most of all, a pattern. I knew in my heart I'd end up with a "yoke" either smocked or a contrasting color. Hopefully, one day I'd graduate to a waist line and big sash – which finally came in the 4th grade. Mother spent most of the summer making my school clothes. If I happened to have a growth spurt, the hem came out and a small decorative tuck was made to hide the old hem line. After nine months in about 3 dozen dresses I wanted to burn them, but she always found a little girl to "hand them down" to.

My good friend, Banny, spent the night with me often and one afternoon Mother saw her underpants while we were swinging. They were white with the prettiest embroidered ruffle around the legs imaginable. Later that week, when I came home from Barret I found 3 pairs of underpants exactly like Banny's lying on my bed. I loved them, but Mother reminded me I had to keep my dress down and not show them to anyone!

My high school clothes were mostly blouses and skirts. I was taught to buy several print fabrics that had the same basic colors for skirts, and solid colors for blouses. Buying 4 of each I had 16 different outfits! What a wardrobe after the WAR! But I still yearned for just ONE "store-bought" dress. It happened in the 8th grade at Easter. Mother got an eye infection and off to Mrs. Bufkin's for my dress. I made sure I asked for forgiveness on Easter Sunday!

Styles were interesting in the late 40s. Hems dropped to 3 inches above our white socks line. The skirts were pencil slim. If there was no pleat at the hemline you'd be late for class. Angora sweaters were hot items. Mary Catherine and Pat had the prettiest, but you had to be careful – they would shed on you and your friends. The white fingertip wool coats were sooo beautiful. Church friends, Phyrne and Janie, got theirs first, and I refused to wear my blue coat. My parents finally bought mine. I've admitted I was spoiled rotten – but loved!

For sports and fun we wore blue jeans with the cuffs turned up several times. Looked tacky then and still does – saw the same style last week!

And then there were the Christmas dances. We had 2 weeks vacation which meant about 12 dances held by different clubs. At that time I had more formals than Sunday clothes. After Thanksgiving Mother would make 3 new formals and redesign, remake, rearrange the 3 or 4 in the closet. We did love to dress me up. The only problem was – would I get invited to the dances?

Our house was heated by floor furnaces on which I stood before my dance date appeared. The hoop skirt under my formal held that warm air until the first intermission.

When I started cleaning out my closet today, my memories drifted back to Mother, which prompted this article. She also would be telling me, "Give that away, it's 10 years old!" We are too attached to certain pieces of clothing to cut the yarn, but do it anyway. The Salvation Army and perhaps your church would be grateful.

Cold weather's coming but SHARING feels better.

PEARL HARBOR

Remember when we were in history class and had to memorize wars by dates, affects, effects, causes, battles, etc? Well, I finally connected to all those demands and details when Japanese aircraft bombed United States territory Pearl Harbor. Even tho my understanding was years later.

It was Sunday, December 7th, 1941, and we were having company for dinner. I had on my new Sunday navy blue dress made by mother and all was right in the Sherrod household. I honestly can't recall if President Roosevelt's announcement was before or after dinner but as soon as we heard it we were all gathered around the 3ft. high Emerson radio. Everyone found a seat, Kiki came in from the kitchen and we all sat stunned trying to figure out just how each of us would be affected.

No one moved until the President finished his announcement. Mother turned out the dining room light over a set table as if time was standing still. Kiki and Daddy helped guests with their coats and as they left said little more than their good-byes.

When we took Kiki home she hugged me goodbye I felt her heart beating extra fast □ just as mine was. Neither of us knew anything about war, but we would learn in the next 4 years.

From that moment on I only have a collection of incidents of great importance which I don't want to forget. I'm sure each of you has your memories. The only thing I learned _that_ day at the age of 9 was that WAR is BAD and UNCERTAIN.

Since Orvis is 10 years older I asked what his Dec. 7, 1991 was like. "During the summer of 1941 we read about the war in Europe with Hitler hoping that America could stay out of it. In September I went back to college for my sophomore year. That Sunday my friends and I had gone to a picture show and as we came out we heard the news. We gathered at the K.A. house and began talking seriously. What would we do? Listening to H.G. Kalten Borne on radio we were educated as to the process it took to declare war and what it meant to our country and us. What would WE do? Being very patriotic we were eager to serve and fight for our country□we were ready to go to war.

" Our decision" – was it the Army, Navy, Marines, Army Air Corp. or what? Who would be eligible, where would we train, would we be together, if we went to war would we survive, were a few of the millions of thoughts in our heads and hearts. We would be making lifelong decisions for 19 year old's futures. We stayed up late that night listening to the radio and waited for the news boys on the streets calling, "Extra, Extra, Read All About It."

Throughout my life my friends and I have talked about a zillion topics: weddings, childbearing, in-laws, recipes, houses, spouses, etc. These all come under an umbrella with each being different. But December 7, 1941, gathered us under a common umbrella sheltering us against a huge tidal wave. We all endured sacrifices, shortages, losses, inconveniences and much more, but we were bound together as a family, city, state, and country. Red white and blue ran all through our bodies. We stuck together from that day forward with the best super glue possible.

I talked to my neighbor Sandy and she explained from a psychological approach why we remember certain things in our lives so vividly. It is referred to as "Flash Bulb Memory"; an intense memory of photographic quality, which is culturally important and "brands" itself on a person.

Wars have to be fought by young men because they see themselves as invincible. Thankfully all my relatives have survived the various American wars. We have never had to experience that kind of loss, grief, or despair. Over the last 56 years many of our friends have lost family members in the wars and remember them daily. "To live in the hearts of those we love is not to die".

SPECIAL SUNDAYS

Remember when going to church each Sunday morning was different from the other days. At my house we had hot cakes which were a real treat. Mother made mine 2 inches in diameter placed on a stack about 3 inches high. What a chore it was to eat just one at a time.

Daddy would announce at the table that we would be going out to "dinner." Our choices were varied so I'll explain the differences.

My Sunday and week-day favorite was Morrison's Cafeteria* which doesn't reflect its charm, food, or great adventure. Mother was active at Kings Highway Christian Church and seemingly the last one out of the door. On our way to town Daddy would begin his same story. We've got to "beat the Baptists." To explain, the First Baptist Church on the corner of McNeil and Fannin with a large congregation seemed to enjoy eating at Morrison's as much as Shreveport Catholics and Protestants. Therefore if, you didn't "beat the Baptists" you stood in line inside Morrison's, in front of Harbuck and Womack, Kresses Dine Store, and starved. But - the wait was worth it.

Men in suits with hats in hand, women in Sunday dresses with hats on head, children with their Sunday clothes and manners on all in line waiting for their favorite dishes. As for me everything was good.

The Mirror Steak House, as the younger generation knows it, was not located on Highland. It was born on Louisiana Avenue down the block from the Jefferson Hotel and Union Depot. The restaurant was built in a round structure of glass blocks/bricks of the day and the top half of the walls were glass with booths around the inside walls and tables in the center. We could usually find a table if Mother's visiting was cut short at church and it was too far for those Baptists to walk. The same house mural hanging in the restaurant today galloped its way into the first Steak House. At least that's what I was told. The feast of my visit consisted of Breaded Veal Cutlets with the best white gravy ever, and topped off with Strawberry Short cake for dessert.

Our other favorite Sunday dinner especially in the summer time was Worm's Hilltop Restaurant on Cross Lake. Daddy's favorite comment to us and out-of-town quests was, "Let's go out to Worms' and eat chicken and fish." What a tease he was but that never affected anyone's appetite.

Lazysusan was not a young girl! It was a round revolving tray secured to the middle of each table. Placed on it were relishes, condiments, lemon slices, hush puppies, etc. It only took one time to learn the Lazysusan had to be turned with ease! Fish and chicken were brought to your table as long as you cleaned your plate. No - we did not have worms for dessert! What a wonderful summer Sunday dinner.

When mother cooked at home we had the same thing - in the cold weather we had roast and rice and gravy. She usually put the roast on to cook when she got up and turned the oven off when we left for Sunday school. However one Sunday we were running late and the oven was forgotten. About half way through church Mother jumped up from her seat and said, "Oh God." Had she heard something in the sermon I missed? She ran out of the church. Daddy and I were close behind her when she finally turned around and said, "I left the stove on!" Don't really remember which restaurant we enjoyed that day.

In 1924, The Brocato family opened a great Italian restaurant downtown which I think was the first. My love for lasagna, spaghetti and veal parmesan was born. After the War, Mr. Brocato opened the "Stopmoor" on Kings Highway. He patented his tasteful relish and we ate Wop Salad with every meal. Later Enrico changed the name to Brocato's, but that did not change the quality or taste of good Italian food.

Sitting at the dinner table 2 or 3 times a day was memorable. Sharing conversations is good for everyone, especially families.

Bon Appetite

SUMMER FUN

It's summer – time for fun and games. Someone commented to me recently about the "good old days". I knew what she meant, but I wondered what she was thinking about. We started reminiscing.

Our neighborhood had an equal number of boys and girls. We attended Barret School, but when the first of June appeared we looked forward to every kind of activity possible.

Our friends were like brothers and sisters whose homes were always open. If you fell in a neighbor's yard, you didn't go home. You were nursed right there with alcohol, mercurochrome and a plain white Band-Aid and encouraged to go play, but be careful.

One summer that started out raining, we decided to have a Monopoly game, ending only when the sun came out for a day. We claimed squatter's rights on our big front porch, much to Mother's chagrin. We learned about real estate, going to jail, collecting $200 and bargaining with our friends. I always ended up with the utility companies and I still do – when I write my checks to Swepco, etc.

Our parents joined the Knot Hole Club of the Shreveport Sports baseball team and took us to the games. The next day we mimicked the players, especially the pitchers spitting. Really disgusting.

About three weeks out of the summer we attended each others' vacation Bible schools. We were very ecumenical – Presbyterian, Baptist and Christian churches. I really didn't pick up on any difference in doctrine because we sang "Jesus Loves Me" at all the churches. At night we played kick-the-can. Sounds sorts stupid now, but we kicked the can (better than the bucket) while we ran and hid. Whoever was "it" would count to 100 by fives, kick the can and start looking for the hidden players who would try to beat the "it" to the can upon being found. Sounds confusing, doesn't it? When you realize "it" had to be chosen by one potato, two potato, three potato, four, the whole thing makes perfect sense.

My very favorite summer activity was swimming in the fabulous natatorium on Creswell, which had everything – slides, rings, diving boards, divided areas of depths and a very cold shower before entering. Swimmers were required to wear rubber bathing caps and some people wore rubber bathing shoes.

We vacationed in Miami that summer and I played in the Atlantic Ocean. Guess what? I learned to float. Oh happy day! Until I learned EVERYONE floats in salt water.

If by chance your friends weren't home, parents were busy and it was raining, you could always rely on the most important thing we were born with – imagination. Webster says it's the power of forming a mental image of something not present or never before wholly perceived in reality.

Heck, when I was a girl (as my mother used to say), I thought about being a teacher, wife, mother and grandmother.....and as of June 19, a great-grandmother.

All it takes is a little imagination.

TAKING DOWN THE CHRISTMAS TREE

Remember when Christmas was over and you were asked / told to un-decorate the Christmas tree? It had been in our living room since the 15th of December, having been bought several days before and set in a bucket of water to help maintain its short life expectancy. It took all three of us to accomplish the job of bringing it into the house after measuring to see if it was too tall. Daddy and I always had the idea — the bigger the better! With the tree set in its stand, straight as an arrow, not touching the ceiling, or the walls of its corner home it was ready for decorations. Many of you will remember those little colored lights about as big as your thumb. Daddy insisted we put all 5 strings on and now we had to take them off. (Those were the lights which were all connected so that when one burned out the whole string went off. This could make you lose your Christmas spirit)

Removing the other tree decorations was an important time because it didn't have to be done quickly. You can really enjoy looking and reminiscing about each of them, the balls, old and new trinkets, some made by children, some bought in far away places, some passed down to your family by grandparents — all full of memories of good times.

Mother and I undertook this job and finished it before Daddy got home to take the tree down. I hated to see it lying on its side by the street waiting to be picked up and taken away. I really didn't want to know where, but perhaps it would be of some importance to someone else. Oh, if that tree could talk and tell the other trees how much fun "he" had at the Sherrod's house. (Note: personification means to give human form to an abstract object. I do that a lot and have great conversations with my car, sewing machine, etc. Try it but not in public.) Undressing our tree only took 45 minutes as compared to the 2 hours of dressing. However we enjoyed both chores.

By late afternoon the aroma of pine was no where to be enjoyed, Kiki had vacuumed up every piece left by tree, children, neighbors, and Santa Claus.

Mother and Kiki attacked the kitchen. They stripped the turkey carcass of all its meat to make the best soup. Do we keep the leftovers or throw them out? This was before there were sizeable freezers inside our refrigerators. We ate it and shared with Kiki who hated to go home. With no husband or children she was a member of our family, we loved it & so did she.

I loved placing my presents in my room in drawers, closet, or my dresser, in my bookcase and having them introduced to the old stuff which would be replaced. It came close to encouraging me to clean out a few drawers, but I calmed that urge!

The next 7 or 8 days after Christmas were spent playing with friends. We went to the picture show on a "week-day," had soup (always tomato) and crackers at noon with the neighbors, went to work with Daddy, read my new books, or went to town but not to exchange, thank goodness, just to the library to work on an assignment some mean old teacher gave us because "you have plenty of time." I made myself a promise I'd never do that when I became a teacher.

December has 31 days, and we have only 5 days left until our own 2007 vanishes. Upon close introspection of 365 days, have we made the best of our time? Your days like mine have been spent taking care of spouses, sharing knowledge learned from experience with children, loving and bragging about grandchildren and great-grandchildren, supporting churches and synagogues and donating time and money to boards/charities. We must take time for ourselves making sure that <u>we</u> are happy and well and remembering those who need our prayers in far away places. Most of all we must be thankful for all our many blessings. It's time for New Year's resolutions!

THANKSGIVING

Remember when Thanksgiving was preceded only by Halloween? Thought I'd scream when I saw my first 2007 Christmas trees standing next to a dumb –looking turkey. What was that turkey thinking? "What are all those stupid bright lights doing on a tree I could sleep under? Where have I been? How can I get some shut-eye when I get sleepy! These and a lot of other questions probably were flooding the turkey's brain!

And speaking of brains, who made the display with school supplies, Labor Day swim suits, huge orange pumpkins all being guarded by scarecrows in a red sleigh driven by Santa Claus with Easter Eggs in his bag? O.K. I've made my point!

Thanksgiving crosses all boundries, it's non-denominational and seemingly everyone can find something for which to be thankful. With no gift buying to occupy valuable time it's a day to be with others or not.

My thanksgivings have taken many twists and turns but the following reports the 1940-1950's.

When Shreveport was just big enough to have two public high schools, they were in fierce competition in everything especially football! I know it's hard to believe but the citizens of Shreveport filled the Fair grounds original stadium, because "everyone" was a graduate of either Byrd or Fair Park. If they weren't they would say they were and pull for that school.

The game started at 2:00 P.M. rain or shine on Thanksgiving Day. This was in the Dark Ages when families sat down together and celebrated being thankful – imagine that.

We attended services at Kings Highway Christian Church at 10:00 which meant Mother and Kiki had to have dinner practically ready to put on the table for any number of people.

We'd rush home from church and finish the final fare, like the best home-made yeast rolls in the world. All through dinner Daddy would sneak a look at his watch hoping that we could be on time. Our dinner ended with mincemeat pie topped with whipped cream.

Upon finishing we jumped up, left the table for Kiki, and gathered our gear. That could mean any outside covering agreeing with the weather. As any native reading this will testify – could be sunscreen on fur coats!

Piled in the car my family had an edge on the trip. Since we lived near the Shrine Hospital we were saved from the traffic my friends had to endure from Broadmoor and South Highlands. Kings Highway was the only cross town route. Those people just had to eat faster!

Regardless of who won (I'm lying) it was always a Thanksgiving experience which is still remembered.

Now – tomorrow is Thanksgiving 2007. My day begins this year by taking breakfast in bed to grandson Connor. I did this for my girls on Sundays when they were young – a bribe not to wake me too early. Then it's off to St. Marks for my next to favorite "hymn –wise" service. We'll sing "We Gather Together", "America the Beautiful", and "God of our Fathers". After the offertory an acolyte will hold our nation's flag while we sing the National Anthem AS IT IS WRITTEN. It's thrilling and I can't begin to wonder what is going on in each person's mind and heart.

The last verse is "O thus be it ever, when freemen shall stand between their loved homes and the war's desolation! Blessed with victory and peace, may the heaven – rescued land praise the Power that hath made and preserve us a nation! Then conquer we must, when our cause it is just, and this be our motto, "In God is our trust". And the Star - Spangled Banner in triumph shall wave o'er the land of the free and the home of the brave".

Among my thanks this year are my thanks to each of you for taking the time to read my thoughts and remembrances which include many of you. Where would we be without each other? Happy Thanksgiving!

TRAIN WHISTLES

Choo – choo – choo – whistle and blow! Here in Broadmoor I can hear the train's whistle during the night, and I love it. The pleasant memories remind me of my Dad who was a railroad man – a KCS man to the end.

Our family rode the train from Shreveport to New Orleans and Kansas City and every city in between several times a year.

I still feel like I'm cleaning soot out of my hair. Over the last two or three years, articles in the newspaper and on TV have dealt with railroad wrecks, construction and complaints.

Today's young people can't imagine the railroads' importance to America since that last spike was driven into the Transcontinental Railroad.

At an early age we were educated in railroading by sitting at a crossing as the train whipped by. Either you counted the cars or if you were older you read the names on the boxcars, some of which came from the far corners of America.

Several years ago my friend, Doretha Barnes, and I were attending a party, and in conversation she commented that she and her husband were late due to a wait at a railroad crossing. She made it clear she didn't mind because it was the Kansas City Southern and laughed. She got my attention quickly!

We realized both our fathers had been employed by KCS, a collection of 86 years! This opened up a whole new topic of conversation and connection. Doretha's dad was a baggage clerk for the L&A (later bought by KCS) in Winnfield. He was in charge of every piece placed into the boxcars there. Each piece had to be weighed on a 15-square foot scale, sealed and documented.

What happens to all those things delivered by rail is mind boggling. In the '30s and '40s the railroad shipped almost everything. When old enough, Doretha and her eight siblings worked for their dad at the depot. They washed the insides of the boxcars, especially for the salt from the mine in Winnfield.

All this was done before school and every other day of the year. Since all family members of KCS employees had passes, her family traveled to Shreveport and with saved wages bought new clothes, toys and went to the Strand Theatre – all in one day – when you'd ride the train!

My dad was a typical company man who lived and breathes his job, which was buying lumber and cross ties for the entire railroad. He traveled during the week to country saw mills, but was home on weekends.

I was not the perfect child so starting on Thursday afternoon I might hear, "Just wait until your father comes home." I always wished for two or three more days between Friday and Saturday, but it never happened.

Neighborhood children and I loved going to Union Station on Louisiana Avenue. Those enormous black puffing engines were majestic. Treasures at the depot included red caps, who carried baggage from cars and taxis to the passengers on Pullman cars. Lee, my favorite, bought me peanuts and Dr. Peppers.

During WWII, hundreds of service men changed trains headed for who knows where. The Princess Park building was a "USO", United Service Organization, which entertained service personnel between trains. Many of my friends had the pleasure of going to college on the trains. I've talked to several, but the tales told to me will remain under wraps.

With our family passes we traveled all over America, often spending the night on the Pullman, which is an experience. From the time the porter keyed open the top berth to retrieve the linens, hang the netting, make up the berth and step aside, it was magic.

However, getting dressed and undressed while sitting on a bed with restricted overhead room, behind heavy drapes, is quite an ordeal.

Needless to say it was a challenge. But the best part of a train trip is going to sleep listening to the clickity-clickity of the wheels. It is the most restful lullaby ever because it is telling me I am going on a grand adventure – or I'm coming home.

That's heaven on earth!

WALKING STUDENTS

Remember when…

…going anyplace during the 30's – 50's if you didn't have access to "wheels" meant you had to walk? As I read the funny papers this morning I thought of my dad saying a little bit of knowledge can always be gained from reading this page. Some of the strips shouldn't be there but who am I to make that decision?

I read down to Hi and Lois and the message struck home – walking! After reading and listening to reports concerning school bus problems I have a great idea. Let these students walk.

When I was a child in the Dark Ages, I couldn't wait until I could walk to Barret School. It was a neighborhood school for children living between Linwood (a dirt road) and Line Avenue, and from Stephenson to Jordan. We all walked, rode bicycles, skated or took the trolley from Cedar Grove. Miss Harriet Birdie Bartoff, principal, rules with an iron hand and dared us to be late. Ask any graduate!

My friends, Peggy and Arla Jo, and I met at the corner and usually planned our own after school activities as we walked, Lila, a kindergarten friend, continued our walking friendship to Barret. We met in front of the Fullilove antebellum column home on Samford. In the spring the side lawn was covered with Jonquils and Daffodils. If no one was looking we would each adopt a handful of beautiful yellow flowers and present them to our respective teachers. On the way home we did the same thing and presented a bouquet to our mothers. We were sweet and thoughtful little thieves. Mrs. Fullilove was probably watching from her windows, but she never said a word to us or our mothers.

As we walked to and from school just think what we were accomplishing. We talked about our inner most feelings in complete privacy, fussed about some boy, complained about our parents or giggled like girls do. We shared our whole lives, built lasting friendships, became healthy by exercising and enjoyed God's world.

All these benefits were to follow me all twelve years of my education – plus a few trips to and from Centenary. From the Shriner's Hospital to Byrd High is .9 of a mile round trip. Each school year has 178 days so considering my 8th through 12th grades, I walked 801 miles between 14 and 18 years of age. My goodness, that's child brutality! I could have had my parents arrested. I did complain, but I always got the old tale from Daddy. "I had to walk 5 miles in the snow, rain and heat!" Please – not again. I DID walk to Barret and Byrd in sunshine and rain in a raincoat, carrying an umbrella and wearing those DARN galoshes…!

The rewards of walking then, as of today, are fantastic. Students would be healthier, more respectful of our neighborhoods, friendlier and perhaps discipline would improve. Just think of the money saved by the School Board.

I talked to Judy about her walking experiences in Arkansas which prompted this column. She walked alone over a mile to school. Her parents encouraged her to always walk on the grass in order to save the leather on her shoe soles. She, too, fussed about those galoshes but her feet were always nice and dry.

Judy's favorite "walking to school" day was her birthday. In her heart she knew that the whole world was acknowledging it by the singing birds and beautiful flowers along her path. As an unselfish person, it was an opportunity to honor herself and celebrate her life with loving parents, enjoy God's world and thank Him for being a part of it.

Walking is such a blessing for all of us. If you can't run, you can walk. If you can only crawl, the goal is walking. As we mature, everything changes, but the will to get from one place to another, is innately strong in us as human beings. In my life I've crawled, run, hopped, skipped, jumped and moseyed, but "walking for exercise or pleasure is at the top of my list. Orvis, have you seen my Nikes?"

WHEELS

As I was getting into my car the other day, I noticed a low tire. My To-Do-List did not include a flat so I visited my filling station. It just needed a little air.

I remember the only flat I fixed. I got home to discover it was on backward. I joined AAA the next day. These memories bring up a new subject – wheels. That invention alone changed the world. (I wasn't there, but I've been told.) My recollection of mobility started on my tricycle.

After three wheels I advanced to the two-wheel scooter with a parking stand on the back wheel! Today they have brakes, motors and lights!

Did anyone have a sidewalk bicycle? Mine was small with wheels 12 inches in diameter. It was fun but with limitations because our front walk was about 25 feet long and no public sidewalk.

During the war my favorite wheels were skates with four wheels on each skate. The nice thing about them was that you could take them anywhere.

All of our school years, and after, we enjoyed the public skating rinks. My favorites were on Greenwood Road and the Fair Ground rinks. I'll never forget showing off trying to skate backward and I fell. I couldn't sit correctly for a long time. Not only did we skate to school, but also to the Glenwood Theater, Thomas Field, Williams Drugstore and the A&P Grocery, but only for a loaf of bread.

By this time in my life I had grown my 14th rib. Most parents have forgotten, but it is the rib of independence. I was 13 years old, having attending Barret for seven years; it was time to go to Byrd High. This meant I had farther to walk, because I was too mature for a bicycle or skates.

Now skip a couple of years – big sophomore. I noticed the parking lot was getting a little crowded. The war was over and cars were once again being produced. These cars were driven by students and stayed in the lot all day long – wow, how much fun would that be.

On a beautiful early fall day I spotted the car of my dreams – a convertible! As soon as my eyes fell on it I broke a commandment, the one about coveting your neighbor's things! The "thing" was a yellow convertible driven by Martha Ann, a pretty blonde. Immediately in my mind's eye, I colored her hair black (not gray) and saw myself driving that car. Now that's wheels!

Years ago someone asked me if I had always worn short hair – to which I responded with gusto, "Yes, I'm waiting for a convertible!" About 20 years ago my husband, Orvis, surprised me with a blue Ford mustang convertible. That was one of the most wonderful moments in my life.

As I sat at a traffic light, with the top down, the car next to me was filled with teenage boys. One remarked, "Look at that far our grandmother." It made my day!

Public transportation entered my life in high school. Electric trolleys during the '40s and '50s were very important to students and working people. Student tickets were 7 cents. I'll never forget the line of students standing on Byrd's side of Kings Highway at Line waiting for the Crosstown trolley. Grass didn't grow there for nine months.

Across Kings Highway, at the same corner, were students waiting to go west on the Crosstown – in sunshine and rain, with no heat or cooling. It was an expected challenge and probably was the birth of our sense of humor.

WRITTEN WORD

Remember the saying, "Fool's names and fool's faces always seen in public places"? Let's face it – it's absolutely imperative that we communicate by the spoken word or the written word. Thankfully we have a choice.

Having just wrapped a wedding gift, and great grandson Hayden's christening gift, I tried to express worthwhile advice to the bride and groom and love and encouragement to the baby. I've experienced being a bride and being a mother, but on a 2 x 3 inch card I had to be concise.

The baby card led me to my own baby book. Mother's words were full of love and concern. "Poor little Joanne has chicken-pox at 18 months – I sure hope she doesn't scar." Other comments were priceless, warm, almost written in secret. A prayer for herself to be a good mother was never to be read by anyone else. After all, I met her when I was born, and she was 30 I'd like to believe that she was as happy then as always. It's just fun to "peek in."

In the same box I discovered her "1920 Girl Graduate Book". In it were treasured thoughts of being a senior in Shreveport High School – her hopes, dreams, activities, and meeting my Dad. More impressively written words accompanied gifts and described parties.

Through our early school years we learned ABC, Reading, Writing and 'Rithmetic from books. Later we were introduced to History and Literature, novels, and poetry. We memorized passages, verses, and quotations which were stamped in our brains.

Recently I purchased another beautifully bound edition of "Sonnets from the Portuguese" of 1850. Remember Elizabeth Barret Browning's words, "How do I love thee, let me count the ways"? Read a couple more of her sonnets, and you'll jump up and kiss your spouse! Written words are encountered everywhere and are directions for every act in our day. We couldn't exist without them.

In grade school Autograph books were strictly a girl thing. We took them to school and asked our friends to sign them. The responses were unique. Remember: You are 2 sweet 2 be 4 gotten? We also had teachers sign them plus any famous person who might come to Shreveport.

The first obvious words and letters for children were road signs – a lesson on reading and checking for glasses. Burma Shave posted priceless highway signs. "Soughest whiskers in the town, We hold'em up, you mow'em down" – as the written word!

Mother kept a guest book for special occasions for which she enjoyed the preparations, the event, and even cleaning up with Kiki. The book wasn't fancy but the names and comments recorded are priceless. Daddy bought a 25 acre farm named Hickory Sticks on Ellerbe Road where thousands of hours were spent entertaining hundreds of guests. One elderly lady scribbled "we would have had more fun if it hadn't been 98°. My homemade ice cream melted before I could eat it" – the written and never forgotten words!

One huge collection of the written word is yearbooks – a true treasure! Orvis refers to my 2 Holy Scriptures as the Bible and the Gusher! Last summer I was asked to write a birthday letter to an old and faithful friend who was terminal. Talk about the importance of words! Friends since Byrd I had a lot to say. My 1948 Gusher spoke her words to me and I found she was that same special friend through the years. I was so grateful and fortunate to be her friend for 59 years.

We can forget the spoken word if it is not too painful but what about rereading love letters, Christmas cards, the Bill of Rights, legal papers, warranties, no fishing or swimming, the written note passed across from desk to desk, and obituaries?

It is only through words written with heart and pen that we find peace, solace, enlightenment, wisdom, and sadness that's buried inside. It's a collection of feelings on paper to act as a reminder of days and weeks of precious moments gone by.

ZEPHYR ROOM

Remember when you made a mistake and someone called to correct you? Seems I'm guilty of ignoring the reputations of several old Shreveport eateries by excluding them. My list is by no means rated - just remembered. I'll do better!

Each restaurant I mention had its special attraction to me. The smallest was the Toddle House, situated on the corner of Murphy and Fairfield. The menu was a typical short-order ending up with the best chocolate pie in Shreveport. Banny and I would ride with her aunt Lolabelle Barrett, to pick up her uncle, Bill Barret, at Princess Park where he played tennis. As we left Barret Place Banny and I would start talking about how good chocolate pie would taste. That's all it took- after 8 blocks we were turning into the parking lot. What a treat – any time day or night - chocolate pie and a big glass of milk.

Two outstanding hotels in town stood back to back - each facing opposite sides of a downtown city block. With the Washington facing Edwards Street, the Youree facing Market Street, and it had the most beautiful lobby staircase I'd ever seen. MGM should have featured it in one of their films.

Peacock Alley, which joined the hotels, was a beautifully papered wide hall with a marble floor. Shops opening off the street also opened into the Alley. There was a barber shop, beauty shop, tie shop, airline ticket office, ladies boutique and the famous "Little Grill" with one long counter serving short-order food.

Entering from Peacock Alley you would step into an "AI" Restaurant. Originally named the Fountain Room it accommodated 150-200 diners according to Shirley and Lionel. When they "stepped out for the evening they headed for the Zephyr Room and were greeted by Swartzi, the Maitre de. After being slipped $5 he would put them at a table next to the dance floor. And what dancing – all the Big Bands coming through the South would be sure to book Shreveport's Zephyr Room. Perry Como, Tony D'Tardo, Harry James and others provided great dancing music.

The Zephyr Room was THE place to go for any special celebration. Alice remembered the lady parties, graduation, birthdays, bridal showers during the day and rehearsal dinners, young men and women making memories and older couples "remembering when". My family was enjoying an evening when I was allowed to remove my shoes so that I could stand on Daddy's shoes while we "danced". What a night! Anytime a special occasion arose the next words would be Zephyr Room. Shirley reported that Muriel Selber's all pink wedding was held there. If only the walls could talk.

When attending the Zephyr Room proper dress was expected. Men always wore suits and ties and at lunch ladies wore hats, beautiful dresses, hose with seams (horrible), high heels, and of course carried/wore gloves.

The ambiance was outstanding. The tiered restaurant was very formal - starched white clothes and napkins, candles at night compelled you to be on your best behavior at the table and on the dance floor. After my first visit I knew the Zephyr Room must be the local edition of New York City life. (which I'd never seen except in picture shows)

The food was delicious. Alice loved the chicken a la King served in crisp pastry shells and Shirley's favorite was Shrimp Remoulade – all of which was served on the left of the guest and removed from the night. And prices!! Frances recalled that it only took $10-$12 for an outstanding Zephyr Room night for 2, dinner, dancing and just being there.

We all love to be entertained be it a little girl tea party, picture show date with your crush, but the best was an evening at the Zephyr Room! Bon Appetit!

ARTISTS

Remember when we memorized quotations in school which were meant to enlighten, encourage, and excite us? Two favorites are "Beauty is in the eye of the beholder" and "A thing of beauty is a joy forever". Beauty can be applied to animals, vegetables, or minerals, but I'm thinking of painted canvases in homes and especially Shreveport galleries.

My first exposure to canvass art was a distant cousin, the dioramas at Louisiana State Exhibit Museum built in 1937. My first visit was before I started to school. It was a place to go on Sunday rides, and it was air-conditioned!

Most impressive are the huge frescoes on the front entrance depicting "allegorical figures of Louisiana surrounded by agricultural, industrial, and cultural pursuit" addressed by the dioramas which emitted appropriate sounds of oil derricks, pigs, tractors, chickens, etc. Going home in a hot car was made enjoyable by discussion of what we had seen. These have lasted through my life, my grandchildren, and my great-grand-children.

Speaking of grandchildren (4 and 6) Scott and Christen needed to become affectionados of the arts. A friend's show at Barnwell would be their first experience. I instructed them on their behavior to be observant, quiet, and thoughtful. Their assignment: Separate and alone choose three pieces which impressed you the most. Do not hurry, and I'll take you to McDonald's --- an honest bribe!

I sat quietly for ten minutes while these little people strolled, after conferring and finally making their choices. With Christen, who is very girlie, her choices were as expected – very bright colors of flowers, houses, etc. Scott's were still lifes regardless of colors ---- food! Watermelons, grapes, apples, etc., etc. McDonalds was next – a promise is a promise!

In 1947 there was a beautiful wooded area on Southfield Road with a posted sign "Future Home of Norton's Museum". We waited and waited until 1959 when work began and completed in 1961. Opened for public viewing in 1966 we could hardly wait to see what treasurers were hidden behind closed doors. During my first visit I fell in love with America through the eyes and hands of Fredericks Remington and Charles Russell as did Scott. Other collection of tapestries, Wedgwood, Audubon – all awaited me to appreciate and savor. The constant changing color canvass of azaleas in the garden has been the background of pictures of my children, grandchildren, grandogs and friends. Inside and outside can't be beat – that's Nortons!

Jean Despujol's collection at Meadows Museum, painted in 1936-38, recorded the lives and times of French Indochina. Enduring many obstacles they came to rest in a Shreveport bank vault until our eyes beheld them in 1975. Those eyes of his portraits mistified me. My favorite, "Hieu" is of a 17 year old peasant girl. A copy hangs in my entrance hall and greets my guests and often reminds me to calm down and enjoy life.

In my museum musing I'm amazed what people can do with a brush, pencil, chalk, or a finger. The talents of Karla, Michael, Joan, Rosemary, Jan, Nena and Charles Ravenna amaze me and provide me pleasure on which I can reflect upon my inward eye – at will.

I must admit the greatest canvass I know is God's ever changing gift --- the sky. One occasion a friend and I sat on the hill in front of Hamilton Terrace School. Resting back we began looking up into the sky. It's amazing what you "see" when you aren't "looking". Our eyes rested on clouds as horses, castles, faces and things which aren't ordinarily "up there", but that day we saw it all.

When we moved to the country I learned two things – how dark night was and how big the sky was. I knew it was there but living in tree – studded Shreveport my view was blocked. A ride down Youree Drive will prove this.

The sky is awesome, enjoyable, unexplainable, and sacred. This canvas is different wherever you go. The sunsets, sunrises, a threatening thunder cloud, one sunbeam shining through a cloud, just sitting and watching the change to a vast range of colors --- unbelievable!

Genesis got it right when God said, "Let there be light", - and he saw that it <u>was</u> good". Amen

BROADMOOR

Remember – home is where the heart is. I love Broadmoor. When I reached the age of realizing where we were riding on those Sunday afternoon treks I decided Broadmoor would be my choice when the time came. My deepest desire was old Pierremont, but in those days parents bought houses according to what they could afford. Imagine that!! My friends Betsy and Belmore had homes in Pierremont which were always open to their friends. Daddy pointed out that they lived on unpaved asphalt streets as I did on William Street. He was a very wise man.

Our Sunday ritual was Sunday school, church, heat the Baptist dinner at Morrison's, Daddy's nap, finish reading the paper and hop into the car for a ride. The car was full of constant conversation on complete silence—just a normal American family enjoying time together.

Our friends Maude and Jake King and children Janie and George lived in Broadmoor on Ockley and was one of my favorite stops. Being a 2 lane asphalt road there were houses on the north side and cotton fields on the south. Sometimes I can still see Shreveport in my mind's eye of how it used to be – then I wake up and see reality.

During our summer visits there was always a watermelon in the King's ice box or plans for homemade ice cream. Janie and George and their neighbors joined in to kick the can, catch lightening bugs or hide and seek until we were ready to go home.

Past the corner of Ockley and Youree Drive to Belmead Street became our first home in 1959 which was the last street in Broadmoor. Across Youree Drive was a shopping center to die for. With Anne on her tricycle, Liz in the stroller we shopped more than necessary. But—it was the place to go: Big Chain grocery store, S & Q Hardware, Morgan and Lindsay Dime Store, Pepper's Drugstore and Pharmacy, Interiors Furniture, White's Cleaners, a Barbershop, Donut/Bakery shop, and Maybe a liquor store! All on top of sandy loam soil. What you couldn't buy there you didn't need.

Out of my back kitchen window I watched Youree Drive Junior High become a reality from foundation to rooftop. There was only grass between us and its final construction.

Past the school St. Luke's Methodist Church of which we were members broke ground for its new plant. The minister was our college friend Tracy Arnold and wife Sue, who advised us we had no reason to be late – now.

Just think, when I married my cotton farmer Youree Drive/Hwy I was only a two lane asphalt road with no street lights except at the 70th street intersection. That road (with no moon out) was black as pitch. With rows of cotton 4-6 feet high standing at attention on each side. Carrol Fiest's land was on three of the corners with the Querbes on the fourth. Gordon Van Hoose's farm followed by Webb and Webb plantation, Ellerbe Plantations, the Whittingtons, Gardners and down to Robson Cupples Plantation. Cotton, cotton, cotton, in different stages in perfectly straight rows producing buds which opened to pink blooms and eventually they burst open to balls of snow white, cotton—and it was King!

As we drive down Youree Drive/Hwy I now we are amazed with the progress and abundance of the variety of businesses specializing in every need for human beings and animals from birth until death. There are several religious denominations, schools, hospital, nursing home, medical resources, grocery stores, clothing, and especially restaurants. When I look at the sign in my kitchen window which Lila bought me, "cooking makes you ugly," my immediate reaction is – Youree Drive!

Thanks to Bob Adams for selling us this house in Broadmoor. For 38 years we've met wonderful neighbors, enjoyed the convenience of shopping, schools, churches, and excellent soil for flowers and gardens. And we appreciate the efforts of Mr. A.C. Steere who named his subdivision after his family's favorite vacation spot—The Broadmoor Hotel in Colorado Springs, Colorado. It's beautiful and cooler, but I like Shreveport's Broadmoor better.

CENTENARY CHOIR TRIP TO NEW YORK CITY

Remember when we acquired a new calendar and quickly flipped through it to find Washington's birthday, Valentines Day, Good Friday, Easter, Memorial Day and Bingo- July 4th? Now that was a holiday! Everyone had a day off. I could smell barbecue sauce cooking the minute I woke up because we always had a party with all the trimmings- right down to the watermelon with the "seed spitting" contest to follow. Whatever you did or will do it's the one we Americans must treasure the most- the fourth-of July! It's really just one word. I've had 76 of them, but the one which is most memorable I'd like to share with you.

As a member of the Centenary College Choir it was our privilege to attend the International Lions Convention each year. In 1954 the meeting was held in New York City the first week of July. Traveling by bus the 49 singers, 2 pianists, and Cheesy Voran our director enjoyed the roads over mountains, rivers, and farm lands. Some choir members had never visited this country with such a close-up view.

Of course New York City is an adventure in itself, and our experience was never to be forgotten.

Madison Square Garden at that time was a huge convention hall, probably seating 45,000. The night of July 4, 1954 was magical with each state's representative marching in with its flag- All 48 of them. The trail of flags circled the entire floor before being placed side-by-side around the apron of the stage. The orchestra chosen that night was Phil Spitalmi's All Girl Orchestra. Far from girls these were about 40 beautiful women dressed in gold dresses playing symphonic instruments. And did they play when accompanying each flag bearer with his state's song!

On the floor in front of the stage and flags was a huge apparatus called the Dancing Waters. It was composed of about 20-30 fountains which flowed in different directions, patterns and heights. I'm sure you've seen them at other locations.

Behind the orchestra the choir stood on risers and provided a very attractive sight as captured in the New York Times.

This was quite an adventure for the choir members especially singing to a huge audience with a wonderful orchestra in New –York-City!

The "grand finale" was to be the National Anthem sung by ALL. As Phil Spitalmi raised his baton for the first note a flag as large (in my eyes) as a football field dropped down from the ceiling amidst so many ohs and ahs that the first notes were completely drowned out.

Personally, I couldn't breathe, much less sing. Finally I composed myself and the lump in my throat and did something I wasn't supposed to do. I took my eyes off Mr. Spitalmi and looked into the eyes of members of the audience. They were holding shoulder to shoulder, wiping tears from their eyes, clutching their hearts, saluting, and standing taller than they thought possible!

With the flag waving in the air, the water fountains rising and swirling, the women playing their instruments, and our choir trying to lift our voices and sing the pride we felt, this July 4th, 1954, was indescribable!

As we began singing the National Anthem everyone joined but as we progressed to the next verses, which most people were not aware of, the opposite side of the footlights became silent with everyone listening intently for each meaningful word. There was complete silence for probably 2 minutes following the 4th verse of our Anthem.

"Oh, thus be it ever when free men shall stand between their loved home and the war's desolation. Blessed with victory and peace may the heaven rescued land praise the power that hath made and preserve us a nation. Then conquer we must when our cause it is just, and this be our motto, In God is our Trust. And the Star Spangled Banner in triumph shall wave oe'r the land of the free and the home of the brave." Amen!

CLEAN CLOTHES

Remember when we listened to radio soap operas which were sponsored by the soap industry? Each had a jingle which you couldn't get out of your head and drove you crazy. For instance, "Young Widow Brown" was sponsored by "Rinse White, Rinse Bright happy little wash day song." OR "Super suds, super suds, lots more suds from Super Suds." OR – L-A-V-A, L-A-V-A for stubborn grime, OR 20 Mule Team Borax- no connection for dirt, OR Ivory which is still 99 and 44 one hundredths percent pure (of what) Can't you see some advertising man (no women then) writing about how happy he was each morning to put on his freshly washed and ironed clothes provided by wife or maid?

Does anyone under 40 realize that washing machines were not in the Garden of Eden? Most houses built in the 20's – 40's had a small room attached to the garage with faucets and outfitted with two #3 tubs. A third was used over an open fire. Kiki had her method of washing while using a washboard with a corrugated rectangular surface. Today it's used as a musical instrument in Zydeco music. What's next?

A week's worth of clothes for a family of four must have been overpowering for Kiki. EVERYONE believed you washed on Monday and ironed on Tuesday (but that's another story). Clothes were divided into different stacks and she washed all day. Whites were treated with bluing which Webster defines as a preparation used in 1669 to counteract yellowing in whites. With no air conditioning I'm sure it helped.

Considering all the work and time it took in 1776 to BE clean, LOOK clean, SMELL clean with bluing, boiling water rinses and wringing the water out after every process with your hands, it's a miracle they didn't go dirty OR join a _____ Colony!

Somewhere in time we began taking our sheets and towels to the big laundry on Fairfield and Common owned by Ben Levy across from Princess Park. We were greeted by a friendly black woman who took our bundle advising us of a pick-up date. Her 2 gold teeth surrounded by her warm smile assured us our laundry was safe, always calling us by name. We were customers until the laundry closed. Another by-gone institution well remembered.

Washing was important but drying was a challenge. Our clothesline had three lines 20 ft long. A sliding bag hung on the line held 2 types of clothespins, the forked piece of wood and the 1846 spring original.

Weather controlled our cleanliness, washing AND drying. "It's going to rain, and the clothes are on the line". Ever heard that? Friend Jay sent the following reminiscent words.

"A clothes line was a new forecast
to neighbors passing by.
There were no secrets you could keep
when clothes were hung to dry.

It also was a friendly link
for neighbors always knew
if company had stopped on by
to spend a night or two.

The line announced a baby's birth
to folks who lived inside
as brand new infant clothes were hung
so carefully with pride.

The ages of the children could
so readily be known
by watching how the sizes changed
you'd know how much they'd grown.

It also told when illness struck,
as extra sheets were hung; (thanks to Ann)
then nightclothes, and a bathrobe, too,
haphazardly were stung.

It said, "gone on vacation now"
when lines hung limp and bare.
It told, "We're back!" when full lines sagged
with not an inch to spare.

But clotheslines now are of the past

for dryers make work less.
Now what goes on inside a home
Is anybody's guess.

I really miss that way of life.
It was a friendly sign
when neighbors knew each other best
by what hung on the line!"
                        Author unknown

     My first trip on newly constructed I 20 was boringly uneventful. Having driven Highway 80 since 1954 I felt ownership and comfort while observing seasonal wildflowers, growth of crops, new homes, painted fences, and reading clothes lines. Nothing was held back, an honest statement of life, clean clothes, and probably clean minds.

     We're reminded that "cleanliness is next to Godliness" by 2nd century Rabbi Phinehas-ben-yair, but it takes hard work and perseverance of body and soul.

DECEMBER 31st – THE END

Remember? You've got to be kidding! Maybe what I played in Summer days as a child, but not what I had for dinner last night. Did I step on anyone's toes? As I've commented before – our memories are our most precious possessions of our being – old or new.

My friend Frances of Barret's and Byrd's 12 years of schooling, called yesterday and played "Remember When". We laughed our heads off! We haven't seen each other for several years since she lives in St. Louis. But there we were, back at Barret playing Dodge Ball and jumping rope.

I always felt comfortable with Frances because in all the school pictures there we were on the back row. If the camera came out we tall girls and boys knew where to stand without being told before the flash- flashed! Growing up being tall has had its advantages except when dating. Bobby, and I had to wear flats and slump!

O.K.- back to Remembering! Today is December 31st. The last day of a year I never thought I'd live to at age 12. In High School we read "1984" so I was convinced we would be dissolved by then. However, we made it and as Minnie Pearl said, "I'm just so proud to be here".

Today closes 2008, and hopefully it was a good year for everyone. Of course there will always be crossroads, Y's in the road, dangerous curves, and pot holes. But it's our road. That's life and our own personal history. When I complained to Daddy about studying history and all those unimportant dates he explained the reason. It's so simple --, "So you don't make the same mistakes, repeat your good deeds, and that you learn your lesson". (NOTE: Words cannot express my joy of writing this column. I've found lost friends and re-lived happy moments!) One of my favorite songs we sang in the Centenary College Choir was written by Joan Whitney and Alex Kramer. I've always wondered about the circumstances of these words.

"I saw the people gather, I heard the music start. The song that they were singing is ringing in my heart. No man is an island, no man stands alone; each man's joy is joy to me, each man's grief is my own. We need one another, so I will defend each man as my brother, each man as my friend". A great lesson to be taught – a great lesson to be learned.

With Mother Nature as a teacher and guide we prepare ourselves beginning on January 1 to greet the next twelve months. With her Four Seasons and appropriate flowers we are challenged with 52 weeks of taking pride in opportunities of volunteering to serve our country, state and city, performing our specific occupations to our best, and 364 days of devotion to our families and loved ones. Of course Mr. Bad travels the same road as Mr. Good, but with God's help we must strive to do our best.

As I reflect on the topics I addressed in 2008, we remembered our national holidays and their meaning whether related to honoring war heroes or religions observances. There were commercial days which reminded us to love Fathers, Mothers, Husbands, Wives, and everyone's birthday. We must keep those connections close to our hearts and practice the Golden Rule with everyone – "Do unto others as you would have them do unto you".

Let's look forward to 2009 with enthusiastic pride and not fall for Scarlet's words, "I'll think about that Tomorrow". Thank God for Today. Happy New Year! From Joanne and family.

DOWNTOWN SHOPPING WITH MOTHER

Remember when we reached the age of really caring what dress – skirt – etc we wore to school, church, or on a date? Compared to today's vast amount of choices we were quite limited. Our mothers had the dependable black or navy blue dressy dress for church funerals, and other important occasions. They learned early during WWI while in high school, and during the depression as a young wife/mother with children that new clothes were close to the bottom of the "I want/need list." They learned to compensate, which is another way of saying, "accessorize" defined as "an object not essential in itself but adds to the beauty of… "I knew when Mother made one of us a new outfit that her next comment would be, "Lets go to town and see what we can find." She loved sewing for us especially in the summer in order that my fittings could be completed. Walking to the trolley we'd make plans to cover as much territory as possible. So many grand stores downtown to enjoy. The big question __ would we "go down Texas and up Milan or vice-versa? Decisions!!

Our favorite accessory was a scarf, made of silk and came in many shapes. There were squares of 14, 36, and 48 inches, triangular, and shawls, in solids, stripes, and prints. I loved the way Mother draped them around her neck or shoulders. She could tie a square knot ten different ways to look beautiful every time. If you didn't want to wear a scarf, colored silk flowers were worn on collars, lapels, and at the waist. They've come and gone for years. A tad of color can bring a ho-hum dress to life. One of my favorite people, Martha Ann does that in the most attractive way possible. She always wears beautiful live flower in a water pin on her shoulder. Her friendly face and God's flower always compliment each other.

Next were gloves – kidleather or fabric. All beautifully made with decorative stitching and cut-outs. Their lengths varied, wrist, gauntlet (below the elbow) and above the elbow. My favorite was white kid above the elbow which I wore one Christmas.

When buying gloves at Hearnes, Selbers, Rubensteins, Sears, Jeans or Goldings you might place your elbow on a small round pillow on the counter while the saleslady put your glove on your hand. If you just wanted to see how the glove might look she would put the glove on a hand/forearm display form on the counter. Those things looked rather weird until I put a pencil between the fingers – now it had a purpose.

We never attended any kind of gathering without gloves; church, funerals, dances, luncheons, cocktail parties, open houses, hospital visits, community concerts or Little Theater. They were absolutely necessary – were they worn? Who knows – maybe in cold weather, but they were always with you!

Next we'd look at hats. All the department stores, less expensive clothing stores, and even dime stores had hat departments. Let's face it – they do make a statement. - "I am who I am." There were even several small hat stores in the neighborhoods; Nancy Nettles, Chez Jere, Mamie Rivet, and my favorite Frances Koch. They even made hats to match your coat or suit! The hats with veils were sexy! Just watch a 30s or 40s movie – Hats come in all shapes; pill-box, fur, garden, cloche, picture, straw, felt, feather, and anything you ordered. My favorite style was worn cocked to one side and pulled down over your eye. Gave me a mysterious look.

Belts were another accessory. Ready – made dresses had self-belts. If you were inventive you replaced it with a complimentary colored ribbon or a leather belt from Kidd-Russ. High school belts were hob-nail 4 in wide leather belts – Cool, but hot in the summer.

Pre-teens to college co-eds were thankfully brainwashed by Mothers as to proper attire. I'm thrilled when Anne and Liz ask advice on "what to wear." SOMETIME they take my suggestion!!

EARTH AND ITS WONDERS

Remember when we took those road trips with our parents and looked at all those beautiful acres of land producing a multitude of wild flowers and trees native to each area? Returning from a Texas wedding I wondered why there were no I20 blue bonnets and who decided that. Indian Paint Brushes, black-eyed Susans, red clover, and purple thistles all brought an array of color.

Later while checking my calendar, I noticed that yesterday was Earth Day. Not being familiar with it I'll explain my personal connection with Earth which has impressed me the most.

My first serious encounter with Earth was at an early age. Peggy and I learned the art of making mud pies. It was a messy job but someone had to do it in order that our dolls would not go hungry. There was a water faucet behind our garage which had a constant drip sufficient to make perfect mud dough. Leaving to dry in the sun we decorated pies with acorns, flowers and berries. There was also enough for a centerpiece much to Mother's chagrin by using her zinnias, roses and lilies. Served on my china tea set outside proved to be a mistake. It was not an outside toy, consequently I didn't serve tea for a long time.

After heavy rains and dripping faucet I had a huge warehouse of worms. They were gross but Daddy who honestly wanted "Jo the boy," taught me to use the sharpshooter and dig deep – and there they were! When you think about worms living in the Earth – how do they know where to go or why? Gathering the worms and placing them in a can my next move was to call my aunt who took me to Cross Lake. She taught me to hook the worms (another gross procedure) and to fish with a hook and cork. Watching fish nibble on the worm while the cork jumped up and down was more fun than catching the fish – which was seldom.

Besides mud pies and worms the Earth corner of Williams and Glenoaks provided our families with food especially during the War years. Our daddies planted a variety of vegetables, never duplicating so that we shared our products to feed our families and were referred to as Victory Gardens. They helped in the overall moral of our country during the War years.

When it didn't rain Peggy and I had to water the plants with a garden hose. Not wanting to pass up a fun opportunity we donned our bathing suits. Talk about mud! We also pulled weeds and often ate sun-warmed tomatoes. Just take a salt shaker and have a seat. What a banquet!

Another Earth source was my sandbox. Mixed with a little water we built houses and roads on which our toy cars would travel. Add a few Lincoln log structures and you have a nice city – or not – when it rained. But then there was always tomorrow. Sandboxes led me to my love of the "Sandy Beach" as my grandchild Christen described it. It's really the icing on the cake/Earth! I was transformed at six, my first sandy encounter. Daddy and I built sandcastles which attracted others and set up a natural competition of the biggest and prettiest. But then the tide proved to be the winner.

Sand exposes itself for all to see, no grass covering its beauty – grain by grain. I'm always guilty of giving life to inadimate things and worry about those tiny grains once produced never seeing their parents again. With the wave's help they're dashed back and forth, sideways and backwards, and up on the beach to rest from their travels.

I love beach walking just as the waves touch your feet with squishing sand between your toes. We make perfect footprints but looking back quickly there's no evidence you were even present. It only takes a moment to realize how insignificant we are at that moment. But do not despair because as you return to family and friends your significance is proven to be priceless.

How can Earth be such a source of delightful, fulfilling, productive and memorable days? Thanks be to God.

EASTER DRESSES

Remember when we were little girls and realized it was Spring? Daddy always quoted his favorite crazy poem. "Spring has sprung, the grass is riz, I wonder where the flowers is." At least it rhymed. Spring brought Easter and thoughts of a new dress, hair ribbon, shoes and basket – all color coordinated. We barely turned around and we were in high school, college, and all of a sudden we were looking for a job. You had turned into a young woman who had new responsibilities – it was the next level, but it was still Spring. It still brought Easter and thoughts of a new dress. We're just women and women have dress thoughts! Let's go shopping!

With many wonderful shops to choose from. I started on Texas Street. I was introduced to "Sue Peyton's" through her daughter Mary Clare who took us there on Saturdays between Morrison's lunch and the picture show. My visits made me aware of "bought ready-made" clothes they were what I aspired to wear! Sue had an overall sense of market buying that captured the variety of women's style, figure, and pocketbooks. The shop's atmosphere was warm, welcoming, and enjoyable. Daughter Frances and her ladies have maintained the original ambiance of the early 1940's. Upscale dressing and wonderful formals and wedding dresses are the specialties. Anne and Liz found their wedding dresses there and Anne's veil was the last one Sue made by hand. (Does it surprise anyone that Mother made my dress?)

Speaking of wedding reminds me of Betty Vicarro whose shop was also an intimate experience. I had planned a trip, saving my teaching salary all year. But along came Ben and I was planning a wedding. Every bride has a trousseau but "made by Mother?" I didn't think so! I had all that money to dispense at "Sue Peyton's," "Betty Vicarro's," and "the Fashion!" Instant gratification provided this bride with a closet which when opened brought chill bumps. "Readymades" were definitely in my future.

Fashion: "the style of the moment among those anxious to appear elegant in dress and conduct." Bobby's parents, the Rosenfields, opened "The Fashion" to a wider variety of merchandise. Margaret King their saleswoman whose personality and dress oozed with style might help you with a complete wardrobe of dresses, suits, coats, hats, shoes, furs, lingerie, and jewelry. This shop was perfectly named because of its high quality of merchandise.

Another wonderful shop was "Goldrings" which had a Tara staircase and could also fill your shopping list. Their Betty Segall in my opinion always stood out as a prime example of the store's personality. Her style, presence, and educated advice to her customers was outstanding. She knew Goldring's stock – what went with what between your shoes and your earrings. Catch a glimpse of her today – nothing has changed!

    Peyton's, Raye's, Naomi Crockett, Bairds, and Centenary Dress Shop were shops operating on a smaller scale of the larger Selbers, Hearnes, and Rubensteins. The quality exemplified in all these was outstanding service but in the specialty shop an intimately warm feeling was expressed by owners on the floor and their saleswomen. We were there to buy and they were there to help/satisfy and please you. Mother and I never had an uncomfortable experience in <u>Any</u> of these wonderful stores. As I've said "down Texas and up Milan or vice-versa!"

    Liz and Anne always had (hand-made by Joanne) precious Easter dresses. When they were little girls they asked, "Why do we have new dresses at Easter?" I explained as Mother had to me many years ago. Jesus at Sunday school had been very sad and upset, but realized that he should come home for a grand reunion with his Father. It turned out to be a wonderfully "new beginning – a new day" not only in his heart but in ours. As a reminder of this celebration we wear new clothes so that looking at ourselves and others we will be thankful for this experience. Amen.

EYES ARE OUR WINDOWS

Remember the children's game "I spy". Obviously it made such an impression on one T.V. writer he chose the title for his award winning program. I'm sure Bill Cosby and Robert Culp had a ball filming it, but if you're even seen Bill Cosby live he probably had hilarious tales about playing it as a child. As I remember the game was played in a confined area such as on the porch when it was raining or in a tree top where spying was "world-wide". "It" chose an object giving identifying hints while the players guessed.

Asked recently by a friend, "If you had a choice as we age which would you give up, your ears or eyes?" It was easy because I chose ears! In my heart and soul I can always "hear" music, voices of loved ones, laughter, and if I choose sadness.

My first education of eyes came in the story of "Little Red Riding Hood". Daddy read it and Kiki memorized it because it was a favorite. Little Red took her grandmother some cookies, but Wolf arrived first pretending to be "Grandmother". Unaware, Little Red entered to find Wolf in the bed and quickly observed, "What big eyes you have". To which Wolf replied, "The better to see you". Thankfully we have two.

Do you remember being in grade school and one of the first things of the New Year was going to the cloak room? I stood at one end, covering one eye, and looking at the biggest E I'd ever seen. Seventy years later that E stared back at me after my recent cataract operation. The whole world has changed everything. Why couldn't they choose another letter just to keep up with the Times? and, why just one letter? Those jumbled up letters could have combined to spell a word and made it easier to pass the test, but – that's the point – it's a test.

Don't know when this test was discontinued, but wish we had been aware that Liz's eyesight wasn't perfect. She began to read road signs that didn't say what they said, and by the next week she was the proud owner of a pair of glasses – hence better grades and reading.
By high school she wore contacts. I was not sold on them, but she assured me they were safe. Frankly I can't imagine sticking my finger in my eye on purpose even if it has a contact on it. I'm just old-fashioned.

As I mentioned my first cataract was removed four weeks ago. Doctor Bruce was marvelous, no pain, could see perfectly immediately, but my other one is a year away from removal. Consequently I'll have to wear glasses only to read before I can obtain my prescription. I bought dollar glasses at my favorite store and now I don't have to remember where I left my old ones. Mother had a similar problem, but she always started the "hunt" in the refrigerator! (that only happened once).

One Sunday as I sat in church I looked at the Minister and couldn't determine if he had 1-2-or 3 eyes! The phone books were off limits, but now this was serious. Called, made the appointment and Don has kept me from buying a white cane! Thank you!

Losing my eyesight would be the end of my world. From AM to PM our world changes as we live and learn. Our eyes are wonderful, but looking into other pairs is thrilling. The first time you see your baby's eyes, Paul Newman's blue eyes, your pet's eyes, crying eyes, parent's eyes and spouse's eyes, they all tell a story. Then someone writes a song –"Some enchanted evening you will see a stranger across a crowded room" – My first time it was across a bridge table, second time across the basketball court! Our eyes are truly the windows of our world.

As a special Christmas gift clean out your drawers and donate old eyeglasses to the Lions Club for their program to re-grind glasses for the needy.

Hopefully we will use our ears to hear and eyes to see how fortunate we are on Christmas 2008! Peek-a-boo! Santa's watching you!

FATHERS

Remember when Father's Day arrived, and we rushed downtown to buy him a new "tie"? Why in the world hasn't some smart designer come up with a new version of a tie? Thankfully there are other gifts today- a new lawn mower , computer, barbecue pit, electric drill- All translate to work which is not really intended but isn't that what Fathers do?

There are fathers, step-fathers, foster-fathers, uncle-fathers, neighbor-fathers which all believe it or not, can be described in the following poem. My friend Judy shared it with me. "Father" 4 years old: My daddy can do anything. 7 years old: My dad knows a lot a whole lot. 8 years old: My father doesn't know quiet everything. 12 years old: Oh, well, naturally, Father doesn't know that, either. 14 years old: Father? Hopelessly old-fashioned. 21 years old: Oh, that man is out-of-date. What did you expect. 25 years old: He knows a little bit about it, but not much. 30 years old: Maybe we ought to find out what Dad thinks. 35 years old: A little patience. Let's get Dad's assessment before we do anything. 50 years old: I wonder what Dad would have thought about that. He was pretty smart. 60 years old: My dad knew absolutely everything! 65 years old: I'd give anything if Dad were here so I could talk this over with him. I really miss that man.

This poem ends where I probably needed him the most – as a grandfather, Anne was 4 and Liz was 2. We all behave by example which led me to discipline my girls as I was. I was to discover how my life had been incomplete. I'd never had a grandfather close at hand, but I sure had one now. How lucky can a young mother be.

My nephew and nieces were older than Anne and Liz so my first-hand knowledge was minimal. However, when Daddy finally got the boy of his dreams in his first grandchild he couldn't have felt more blessed. I was off the "boy hook" so Johnny got "the horse and saddle" and instructions on sawing, hammering, and mowing. Thankfully father John was kind and shared his son with Daddy.

Love cannot be explained between grandchild and grandfather (I found out 25 years ago!) Daddy loved my little girls more than he loved me! When visiting our home Daddy would pass us at the door while calling for Anne and Liz. I finally got used to that, especially when he found them he thanked their parents for them.

Anne was 6 months old when she spent her first night with the Sherrods. However, Liz was 6 weeks old for her first sleep-over. It was a blessing because Daddy discovered her little foot was turned in which led us to the doctor. As a result she walks perfectly and has since she was 8 months old. Since that moment I've had complete confidence and trust in their care and judgment. They aged along with Mother and Daddy, their grandparents.

Since we lived in the country with no neighbors to play with, Anne and Liz were at a loss as to "What to do" after watching Captain Kangaroo. Dadee, as was his grandfather name, built them a playhouse. It was a normal size room 6x6 with a porch for rocking chairs. My emotions were mixed – from "Why didn't I get one" to thank goodness they aren't running in and out of our house. Now Daddy had two more grandchildren to teach hammering and sawing to!

At ages 8 and 10 the over-nights consisted of driving Daddy's 1952 truck up and down the driveway (which I didn't know about), not telling me when they miss behaved, eating forbidden candy, shaving with an empty razor when Daddy shaved, taking them on the KCS train to Texarkana and back in one day and how to make the best oven-toast with homemade strawberry jelly.

I'm guilty of all confessions in Judy's poem. Daddy died at 96, I was 61. I'll always be his baby. I sure do miss those 3 kisses he always gave me on my forehead.

Happy Father's Day to all kinds of Fathers.

FINALS PASSED – GET A JOB

Remember when June 1st came and it was all over – finals passed and on to college – finals passed and on to the outside world. Were we ready for the next level considering how secure we had been? Since birth our lives had been a joy ride. But now at 22 or so it's time to find a job – freedom, no more nag, nag, nag from adults – What bliss! Or as a college freshman at 18 a time of independence – no more nag, nag, nag – What bliss! (Having lived at home during my 4 years at Centenary, I'll relate my experience as a college freshman's mother.)

Everyone is aware that a high school senior is the smartest creature on earth. Then suddenly he/she as a college freshman is the dumbest creature on earth, and it only took 3 months. So much was to be learned involving every part of our being. As Mitzi defined college -It was a time for trust by the parents and trial by fire for the student.

When we left Anne on the dorm doorsteps she was with Karen, her Byrd friend and now roommate. She and I felt secure as I'm sure Karen and her mother Linda did. Help! – the blind was leading the blind in Lafayette and the mothers were crying in Shreveport! From all reports the girls were safe and happy. Both were older sisters which was in their favor. But were the lessons we taught them being used to their advantage? They were there for an education realistically so I wondered if Anne was attending classes as planned. College classes are a heck of a lot different from high school. Having classes in several buildings is a challenge! Scheduling classes MWF or TT at 8:00 or a lab 2-4 TT another challenge! What a job for an 8:00-3:00 student to absorb! And you'd better not miss class.

Anne and Liz had shared a room so sharing was expected. But with a friend, things were different at college. To name a few there was quiet time to study, the telephone, TV, bathroom (sometimes with 20 people) friends, homework, advice, tears, and space in general. Sometimes your roommate is a total stranger! She survived and I barely did!

As for a college graduate challenges were of a more serious nature. It was time to seek employment, possibly moving across the state or country, finding a home and transportation – and always wondering, "Am I making the best decision for me and perhaps a new spouse?"

At 22 I was to be the first college graduate in my immediate family. Mother and Daddy, my proud parents, told me in April, "Don't worry about a job, we'll always take care of you." At my age I was still a spoiled child. I made up my bed, dried the dishes for Kiki, held out my hand for the car keys and money. What a life! However the time came for me to be responsible for myself. I loved Shreveport and home and all they afforded me, but I was a big girl realizing my life was just beginning.

I wanted to be a teacher since the third grade with Annie Merril Graham Scarborough. But my interest was in teaching high school English. I knew if I applied for a Caddo parish job I'd probably be offered one. I had other plans when I read the want ads for the first time in my life. I applied for teaching positions in Denver, Las Vegas, Dallas, and South America.

In late June I heard "Are you looking for a job, Jo?" Then August 1st, "School starts next month!" Never knew what changed their minds.

The next day a Longview friend suggested applying there. I did and got my first teaching job on Friday August 13, 1954. The Sherrods were elated.

Junes and Septembers are full of challenging times for "matriculators." Great holes were cut in my heart that first night of empty bedrooms which I'll never forget. Most of all I missed my goodnight kisses – I still do 32 and 30 years later.

FIRST DATE WAS UNFORGETABLE

Remember when "DATE" became your most important vocabulary word? DATE has several definitions: 1) an appointment to meet at a specific time; 2) "person" with whom you have that appointment; 3) social engagement between 2 persons which after has a romantic character. I was rather sheltered and if Mother had read Webster's, I would not have dated until age 20! Going to Byrd at 13 as 8th graders, we observed those upperclassmen for 2 long years. It was quite a learning experience and until the time I reached the dating age of 15 - couldn't pass quickly enough!

My first big date, at 15, was with (codename) J.C. who asked me to the Football Banquet at Byrd's cafeteria. We always asked our parents permission – probably because they wanted to know with whom, where, and gave me a curfew. Not a bad idea for today's young people. J.C. arrived before I was ready which gave him the opportunity to meet my parents.

We were double dating with seniors! As we turned on to Kings Highway, J.C. drove 20 mph. It was his first date to drive his car! The banquet was fun, but he seemed to be hurrying to the car. Back down Kings Highway to my house, I found Mother and Daddy in the living room with porch lights ablaze. I told him I had a good time, and he practically ran to the car!

At our 50th Byrd Reunion Banquet, J.C. related this entire date to everyone about how my Dad lectured him about driving, being a gentleman, and bringing me home safe and sound! No wonder he never asked me for another date!

It's memories like this which set up 15 as the dating age for Anne and Liz. A month before Anne's "15" Rob Weyman invited her to a concert! But rules are rules! <u>Orvis</u> gave her permission because the two had played together in our neighborhood and, even though he was a year older, he was a "safe date" – we knew his parents!

Upon leaving that night, I casually asked Rob what time to expect them back home. Turning around he said, "Before school starts in the morning!" Oh, that Weyman wit had been passed down! (I stayed up until my baby came home!)

Dating in high school was centered around a variety of activities. Movies, especially on Friday and Saturday nights at the Strand and Don, were where you definitely wanted to be seen with a date. Boys wore sports coats, weather permitting, with nice slacks and maybe ties. The girls wore nice dresses, skirts, sweaters and, certainly, hose and heels!

Hayrides were popular and the regular route was around Cross Lake, stopping at a park for a wiener roast. I saved my allowances and bought a wind-up record player, which was always taken for dancing. The girls wore blue jeans with the legs rolled up 3 or 4 times. Thought it was cute 60 years ago!

For athletic events and casual parties we wore skirts and blouses/sweaters and saddle oxfords or penny loafers with pennies stuck in them!

Our most important dates were the Christmas dances given by our social clubs. Remember the Progressive Men's Club, American Legion and Masonic Lodge on Cross Lake?
The town dances were in the Crystal Ballroom, Querbes Clubhouse, Shreveport Country Club and the Pelican Club in Bossier City. We wore long formals and tux which definitely were an influence on our behavior.

Having a date to a dance didn't mean you couldn't dance with other people. Orvis and his buddies would sometimes go to be in the "stagline" and wait their turn to "tag" in on girls who <u>always</u> came with a date.

Car dating could be very interesting at times. Surprise, we're going to single date – double date – triple date – or quadruple date! The iron rule was – only 3 in the front seat – it was safer that way!

From my point of view, dating has been an enjoyable ride – as a high and college student, teacher and young widow. Dating begins our process of finding that one person who will make us happy and whole for a lifetime. My favorite first dates were with Ben and Orvis – "til death do us part".

FOOTBALL

Remember who, when, where, and why you played football when you COULD play football? My WHO involved all ages of boys and girls in the Sunny Slope subdivision that included any guests we had visiting. If you went to someone's house to play --- you played anything --- rain or shine ---- we were prepared!

The WHEN was any afternoon in September, October, November and December, but mostly on Saturdays when we could field two acceptable teams.

The WHERE was the vacant lot on Kings Highway behind our houses on William and Glen Oak streets. It was the location of all our outdoor sports.

The WHY is that most of our play was centered around "ball" games until Daddy put up the fanciest Badminton court with electric lights leaving room for the croquet set which only came down when the lawn was mowed. Birdies/shuttlecocks and balls and mallets were popular at night. But come day time we were practicing passing a spiral, kicking, and catching flies and grounders. We were all talented in running, therefore we were well-rounded athletes from 6-16 years old. No one was excluded.

All grade schools had school sponsored football and basketball teams, but of course nothing for girls. I used my acquired pitching ability to play Dodge ball hence I was among the first to be chosen for a team.

For some reason I liked football the best although I could never throw a good spiral, that is a talent which I love watching on TV. How can they throw 60 yards to a man running down field with his back to the flying ball, turn around just in time and catch it? I love miracles.

When we moved to Pennsylvania Street the block was full of young aspiring high school football players. One day Dean, Dan, Darrel, Miles, Lee and Butch were playing in the street in front of our house. Their kicked ball landed in our yard so I picked it up and kicked it back. Liz and Anne asked me not to do that again – it was embarrassing!

Another kick I returned was in the Astrodome in Houston. Orvis was visiting for the Independence Bowl so we went to the University's practice – and the opportunity arose. If I were to be asked, "what is the one thing I'd like to do before I die?" I'd say; "Running for a Touchdown". That has to be the most thrilling feeling in the world with thousands of fans rooting you on to cross that goal line.

When I entered Byrd I could hardly wait until the first football game. Fair Park and Byrd, great rivals, were fortunate to have stadiums easily accessible to their schools. Byrd's was on its campus, and Fair Park played on Fair Grounds field.

On game days there was always an assembly with the 70 member uniformed band on stage. The Donkey Serenade by Friml & Stothart was being played and for some reason Mr. Koffman approached Mr. Benner, took his baton, mounted the podium and proceeded to direct the band. The students went wild! I last saw him directing in the fall of 1953. Just a part of football season at Byrd. Some things never change.

During the assembly Anne, Morris, Bobbie and Ernie led cheers, the band played and the entire football team passed by the microphone with encouraging words of winning. This was followed by a handshake from Mr. Koffman and Coach Rowen. With such excitement I hardly remember what transpired until 3:00.

Byrd's stadium stretched from goalpost to goalpost with about 25 rows. Home game played there, Thanksgiving game was at Fair Grounds which involved the whole city. Believe me those Fair Parks Indians had just as much fun with as many wonderful memories as the Byrd Yellow Jackets – just ask Leo!

Mr. Koffman and Fair Park's Mr. Albertson and their coaches encouraged their players to play fair with honesty and unity. Football is only a game played by rules and punished if broken.

My theory is that if you play an honest game with integrity it rubs off on you with your family and friends in the game of life. Hut – 1-2-3 Hike!

FORGET GRADUATION?

Here we are again. It's been 9 months since September – just in time for the "baby to bloom." It's graduation time and with that comes a multitude of functions and important awards to honor seniors of high school and colleges. They're different in every aspect. High school graduation means you'll still be a dependent on Dad's income tax, asking for the car, able to come home from college to wash a month's dirty clothes, and sleep in your own bed while being spoiled by your parents for a weed-end.

A college graduate will have to answer questions like, how's job hunting (the day after graduation), clean up your room the painters and new carpet are coming next week, we can't decide if we need an extra bedroom or office in your "old" room. Help – Is this what matriculate means?

During May in high school we were honored/punished with scads of parties. There were girl parties, boy parties, even you and your date parties which were more fun.

One remains in my memory of the Means family having a graduation party at their antebellum home near Gloster. My date and I were invited to a barbecue. Mother and Daddy gave us orders not to drive too fast on the Mansfield Road. Being in the country for us city people was a neat treat until supper was served – potato salad, baked beans, homemade ice cream and the best barbecue ribs I'd ever tasted – not to be tasted again. Someone made the mistake of asking what kind of meat. With a grin from ear to ear the host boasted GOAT! You could hear us city slickers stop eating – all at the same time. The beans, salad, and ice cream were to die for! Nothing else!

The girl's parties described on the invitation left nothing to our imagination. There were teas, coke, badminton, swimming, minigolf, Betty Virginia picnics, dances and slumber parties. Our appointment books were filled and Mother was sitting at the sewing machine. The dress for these parties was according to the invitation. Viva Begbie reported for the paper the stories and pictures of these parties some of which were casual, most demanded nice clothes. Our group always went together while trading off whose car we'd go in. One afternoon as we arrived at a party in old Pierremont Jane discovered she had forgotten her white gloves – a social sin! I shared mine with her saving the hostess from reporting the incident to her Mother! My how times have changed – but according to the glamour magazines gloves are coming back!

Then there was the wonderful experience of receiving graduation gifts. Mine were placed on the dining room table for public (family & close friends) display. This being the first time to receive all these gifts was very exciting. AND of course having to write thank you notes to each and everyone of which Mother passed her approval.

Popular gifts to this senior of 1950 were jewelry, scarves, luggage, a radio, and handkerchiefs. A porcelain rose powder dish and a copy of Elizabeth Barrett Browning's Sonnets from the Portuguese are still with me – after 58 years! They and I are antiques!

Mother, having graduated from Shreveport High in 1920, had a "Girl Graduate – Her Own Book," leather bound, which covered her life as a senior. There are pictures, a purple and gold ribbon, a personal calling card, gold SHS pin, autographs from friends and Grover C. Hoffman. It says, "After being requested and invited I'll just scribble my name so that in years to come your principal for your last year may not be forgotten entirely. I only hope that all your days will be as happy as the days of your senior year seem to have been. A very long list of friends will watch your future with a great deal of interest. Don't forget – Grover C. Koffman."

To quote Mother this was her most treasured graduation gift. Among others she listed a silver vanity case, pin tray, gold lingerie clasps, and toilet water.

Excitement of the occasion, gifts, parties, honors received, dates, tears, laughter, and our parents – who wants to forget Graduation?

GLOBAL WARMING INVENTED IN SHREVEPORT

Remember when we had never heard of global warming in such an over-rated way? It was long before Al Gore was born. Honestly, global warming/cooling/freezing/sweltering – your choice, were invented in Shreveport and our surrounding areas. I haven't figured out if God was mad at Larkin Edwards, Capt. Shreve, or just plain "tuckered out" the day he created the Ark-La-Tex. Anyway – we locals adjust to many obstacles – weather being one! I love warm weather and despise cold weather. My theory is "I was born naked – been cold ever since" (except at 50 when hot flashes arrived).

I realize that people (Orvis) come from other parts of the country which, believe it or not, have definite seasons! How quaint! But in Shreveport on January 8th as I'm writing, it is almost 80°. If any of my friends had a heated pool I'd call for permission to swim. Then I'd pick up my fur coat from storage because I'll probably need it next week.

My point is that we have multiple seasons at any time of the year! We have to be the healthiest people alive (except for allergies). We are also disciplined to accept whatever weather God sends us. Please keep your swim suit and fur coat in the same closet.

Weather reports on radio and television are very important. Years ago, during bad weather, I always looked forward to Mother's phone calls, "Joanne, do you know what Al Bolton just told ME?" Mother was at home and Al was in the KSLA studio. He always had such a personable and caring delivery – and nine times out of ten he was correct!

I've always enjoyed snow occasionally, but a little goes a long way! When we were in grade school and awoke to bad weather, our family waited for a radio announcement from Roscoe White, Superintendent of Caddo Parish Schools. Finally we got our wish – NO SCHOOL! What a boon. Scheduled tests, unfinished homework or library book – snow was the answer to a prayer. Parents always knew our short comings therefore completion of these tasks preceded play time. How did we survive such strict rules?

I'll never forget the snow holiday when Peggy, my next-door neighbor, called to inform me it was snowing more in her yard than mine! Separated by a fence, she was looking out to Glen Oak Street and I was looking out to Williams Street! We were always in control of that corner – but obviously not that day. Our mothers dressed us head to toe, warned us to be careful and then met in my backyard. Everything was white and we loved it. We threw snowballs, made snowmen, ate snow ice cream and lay on our backs and watched snowflakes fall on our faces and into our mouths. Life could not have been better that day! We took pictures, which I treasure, because the snow was three feet deep – or maybe an inch – debatable!

In high school the snow days Patsy and I remember were in February 1948, our sophomore year. Snow began falling before 3:00, so when the final bell rang the school yard was covered. I wouldn't swear to it, but that's when Thrill Hill was invented! Sleighs were made out of garbage can tops, cardboard boxes and trays. We were an inventive generation!

In January 1951, as a member of the Centenary College Choir, we were returning home by bus from Alexandria on a snowy night. Suddenly a truck appeared to be taking his half of the highway down the middle! Our bus was forced to the soft shoulder and got stuck. After much discussion by Cheesy and C.C., our driver, we pushed that Trailway bus back on the highway!!! Can you imagine? We thanked God for his help and our strength.

Honestly, we can't do anything about the weather but diversity is sometimes frightening – tornados, wind, snowstorms, ice storms, lightning. It's certainly not boring like it must be in Scottsdale or Acapulco. I wouldn't live anywhere else – would you? Then again, Hawaii sounds nice!

GOD BLESS AMERICA

Remember? … "While the storm clouds gathered far across the sea let us swear allegiance to a land that's free. Let us all be grateful for a land so fair as we raise our voices in a solemn prayer … God Bless America, land that I love, stand beside her and guide her through the night with a light from above. From the mountains, to the prairie, to the ocean, white with foam, God Bless America, my home sweet home, God Bless America – my Home – Sweet – Home!" I hope that each of you either heard with your hearts Kate Smith singing with that glorious voice or you sang it out loud. It was written by Irving Berlin in 1918. Kate with this song became the "unofficial second national anthem" during her show November 10, 1938.

Kate Smith's radio show was looked forward to with great anticipation as were H. G. Kaltenborne, Edward R. Murrow and Walter Winchell informing the public of what was happening in the world. They reported the truth because since 1917 we had experienced WW I, the Great Depression and were anticipating another conflict with Hitler and friends. The press was honest in their reporting and did not editorialize. They owed this to the American public because we were/are a strong and loyal people to our beloved America. We, all citizens young and old, need to be privy to the truth – how else could we defend ourselves.

My friends and I were 9 in 1941 and 13 in 1945. I shutter to remember the reports on radio, newspaper, and newsreels at <u>every picture show</u> we attended and seeing all the nude bodies in open graves, the prisoners of war being marched along bombed roads and battlefields strewn with our own soldiers. No – we have not forgotten one moment of those four years. The rationing in America of meat, shoes, gas, shortages upon shortages, and not seeing members of our family in uniform for years --! We were/are strong and brave and full of courage.

Upon entering Byrd and Fair Park as eighth graders in 1945 we looked up to classmates in ROTC uniforms. This helped us to remember the recent past and protect the future. Then came Korea where our friends lost their lives.

Having finished college in 1954 we asserted ourselves as adults and assumed our role as protectors of this great land. We felt prepared.

Thankfully America has retained the habit of keeping our memories fresh by observing special holidays to honor those who fell on "foreign land" in order to keep "our land" free from enemy forces. Memorial Day, since 1868, remembers Civil War soldiers and Veteran's Day of November 1918 celebrates the armistice signing ending the Great War (WW I). Thankfully the Fair Park and Byrd ROTC units honor this day with an assembly and military inspection. (If travelling down Line on Greenwood Road check out the uniforms on the school's front yards on November 11, 9:30.

Celebrating the bravery and courage of our fallen Americans in best acknowledged in the national cemeteries: Arlington, D.C., Normandy, France, and Punch Bowl, Hawaii where we stood as Orvis explained his naval duties in the Pacific WW II with tears in his eyes – 30 years later! He tells me today, "If I'm needed, I'll go – at 86". That's the deep love we Americans have and we promise, "I pledge allegiance to the flag of the United States of America and to the Republic for which it stands, one nation under God, indivisible with liberty and justice for all".

Today, Tuesday, October 27, I'm wondering who will be our next president?

My prayer is that he molds his term by the last verse of our national anthem. "O thus be it ever when free men shall stand between their loved homes and the war's desolation!" Blest with victory and peace, may the heaven – rescued land praise the Power that hath made and preserved us a nation! Then Conquer we must, when our cause it is just, and this be our motto, " In God is our trust." And the star spangled banner in triumph shall wave o'er the land of the free and the home of the brave!"

God Bless America, my home sweet home!

GOOD NEIGHBORS

Remember when… we didn't have an air conditioned house? In order to keep cool we had to open the windows on opposite sides of the house to enjoy cross-ventilation – plus cross conversation/information. We were aware of our neighbor's news because sound carries perfectly with the evening breeze. With that in mind we were quite intimate with our neighbors.

Now, however, some people hardly know the names of their "people next door." Webster defines neighbor as "one living or located near another." That's a rather icy definition as far as I'm concerned OR Webster lived in the country and didn't have neighbors – Pity!

As for my young life of having neighbors I couldn't have been more fortunate. I've talked about Peggy from next door, Arla Jo from down the street, the Boutes next door on the other side and several other boys and girls. With this band of mischief-makers we played badminton, croquet, climbed trees, and swang in my yard. In the lot next to Peggy's we played baseball and had "stilt" races, at Arla Jo's we put on plays because her garage door was on rollers and provided a perfect stage and moving curtain.

Frankly I don't remember a misunderstanding amongst us but if so they never lasted long enough to get home to tattle! We all felt comfortable being corrected by someone else's parent – we were just "neighborhood children" feeling a sense of belonging, loyalty, and dependency or/for each other.

During the summer months we checked out the neighbor's kitchen to decide where we would claim "squatters' rights" close to noon. After all if you had company it was only good manners to ask them to dinner. (We ate dinner at noon and supper at night!) Just think of all the stuff we ate never looking at a label, calories or not – gosh, and here we are still kicking and hopefully feeling pretty good!

It's interesting to note that our neighborhoods involved more than "your" street. The correct definition, and it's mine, was anywhere I could reach by walking, skating, or riding a bike – just be careful crossing the streets. As I reflect on this by today's standards it might have been parent brutality. However I and everyone else in the 30's, 40's and 50's in Shreveport survived.

Daddy always said good fences make good neighbors. Over the back fence was a nice Italian couple who had a set of twins. The father worked long hours and the mother seemed exhausted all the time. I learned to walk the top fence board and finally made friends with the mother. Asking if I could play with the babies she almost hugged me to pieces. I probably was in their house 4 times a week for the next 10 years and 2 more babies. Just think if I hadn't taken such good care of those children Joe and John Fertitto, Agatha and Mickey would never have been so successful. I take full credit with Sam and Florence!

As a young couple and mother, started our family life next door to the Browns. He worked as a new car salesman and came home in a different car every afternoon. Anne at 4 would say "here he comes in another new car" as she watched her Daddy's truck turn into the driveway! Mrs. Brown was my confidante, cooking advisor and always a helping hand.

Then came the move to the country. As I've said, for a city girl the transition was difficult. Ben went to work, Anne went to school, and Liz sold driveway rocks to our farmer neighbors who joined us for lunch coming from Lucas, Robson, Caspiana, Ellerbee Road, and Bossier City. Now do you know why I hate to cook?

Moving back to Shreveport and marrying Orvis we found our own neighborhood – 19 homes on our block with 15 teenagers! They were ecumenical, fun-loving, and respectful. They've all grown up to be adults, mothers, fathers, professionals, but still our loving little boys and girls.

We've been taught to "love thy neighbors as ourselves" which is sometimes difficult. But we ask HIM to "fill us with love, show us how to serve the neighbors we have from you."

Peace

GRANDPARENTS

Remember when your parents said, "Let's go see your grandparents?" I wasn't that fortunate. Daddy's mother died when he was 9. His dad remarried Miss Mary, as his children called her, and she was a wonderful step-mother to her new family. Living in Alabama provided my family with a once a year visit with them.

Mother's mother died when I was 3 and her father died a few years later. So realistically I was deprived of "over the mountains and thru the hills to grandmother's house we go."

We learn by watching others perform and by doing – everything. My sister's children were born when I was in high school and college while I was living at home. My "grandparent schooling" was first hand and most enjoyable.

Johnny, the first grandchild and a boy, could not have been born into a more anxious grandparent situation. Daddy finally had his boy, with Sherrod for a middle name, who couldn't get out of that bassinette quick enough for his grandfather. His other grandparents had 3 sons so they were quite willing to share. It took the pressure off of me and Daddy started calling me Joanne instead of Jo.

Years later Johnny had 2 sisters, and I learned first hand what Grandparents were, what they stood for, what that kind of love was, and placed it in my memory bank for the future I hoped I'd have.

My parents were renamed for proper identification. My sister and I called him Daddy but Johnny called him Dadeē. We called her Mother but Johnny called her Fō Fō. Next came my children who accepted Dadeē, but Mother became Momma. Since we were aware of who was who now – "let the games begin."

Being grandparents was the high point of the Sherrods' lives. Love them, spoil them, and send them home! At 6, Johnny received a horse for Hickory Sticks. Anne and Liz at 6 and 4 got a 6x6 foot playhouse in the country. Nothing was too good for his grandchildren. Mother's contributions were hamburgers, blackberry cobblers, and swinging while repeating, "How do you like to go up in the air," plus a million more memories.

Then came our grandchildren. Susan's, Erica, and Dru who named us Dō Dō and Coach (that's another story) Sally's Beth and Christopher who kept the Dō Dō and added Granddad, Anne's Christen and Scott and Liz's Connor, kept the Dō Dō and added Granddaddy.

It's just so much fun when these little people grow up and are capable of carrying on an intelligent conversation. It doesn't make any difference about the subject, but watching them make complete sentences and thoughts is just a miracle.

Telling them stories is so much fun – true or not. If you believe the veins on the top of my hands were full of chocolate syrup running thru my body so be it. They share their Easter rabbits with me quicker.

While babysitting with Christen and Scott I took them to the Barnwell Center's "Enchanted Garden." On the way I told them about a magic gold fish which had a white square on its head. Well, we found one in the Barnwell fish pond. Each of us made a wish and threw a dime into the pond. On the way home Scott told us he wished he could be 7 years old. And guess what, it came true 3 days later. Miracles never cease to amaze me. I hope he has fun with his little boy.

As young parents we don't get instructions when these babies are born. I was at a loss but Mother came to my rescue by teaching me how to Mother. She in turn was learning how to grandmother. The trust between us was unbelievable. Through the years I've called upon their experience, wisdom, and most of all availability. I couldn't have survived without them. Daddy filled the void when Anne and Liz lost their father until Orvis came into our lives.

Parents are probably the most important teachers we have. We learn to act by observation from one generation to another. We're doing the best we can and hope we'll be remembered for all the fun we've had as Dō Dō and Coach/Granddad/Granddaddy.

HICKORY STICKS

Remember when we referred to Haynesville as Haynesville, Louisiana? My how times have changed! As Daddy used to say, "God doesn't make land anymore, once you buy it it's yours on loan from God" He's no longer with me, but I'm sure he wishes he'd kept the mineral rights when he sold his beloved farm.

In 1948 25 acres of woods were purchased at Ellerbe and Leonard Road's, intersection. When this was announced at the supper (not dinner) table Mother raised her sweet voice and screamed, "I'm not leaving William Street!" Her outrage was calmed and assured – that would never happen. Daddy was raised in the hills of north Alabama and had yearned to own land and play farmer again. His dream had come true – let the games begin!

First things first – the place needed a name. Being in the timber business and familiar with different species he discovered Hickory trees dominated. After much discussion with our family the name was chosen, "Hickory Sticks."

Next step was a long list of cosmetics: a fence, a road from Ellerbe to the top of the knoll where he already had plans for a house and a pond. Soon with the help of friends the acres were surrounded by a barbed wire very taunt fence. A perfectly graveled road started at the entrance with a huge white sign raised for all to see "Hickory Sticks – Private Property." This tree farm filled the place of the boy he always wanted but also included me on occasion.

The biggest endeavor was building a pond. Daddy visited parish offices for planning and digging the acre hole. Thinking ahead he visited the library looking for proper types of fish which would be compatible with all the requirements for fishing/catching/cooking on site/eating. I've never seen him so excited!

I don't know if his KCS job suffered from lack of attention, but knowing his personality he probably found another day to accomplish all his long awaited plans.

Pond completed and stocked, next step was a pier, a long pier to accommodate everyone. It could have been described as one for which Noah was seeking.

My parents lived close to Holsum Bakery which sold stale bread which they bought and headed to Hickory Sticks. Walking around the pond they cast the bread upon the waters to the fish. The rustling of the water resembled natural fountains. Weeks later we caught the fattest brim imaginable, and were they tasty!

Next on the list was a cabin. After much research and communicating with the right KCS people he bought a "workmen's rail car." You've probably noticed them on a sidetrack. They are easily recognized because they look like box cars with doors and windows. Upon delivering it on the winding road it finally came to rest on top of the chosen knoll. It was a castle which tripled its size by having screened front and back porches added. His dream became a reality.

The Sherrods had always been gregarious people – church, bridge, canasta, neighbors – who enjoyed their get togethers. Now they could explore the outdoor adventure with the lake which was quite often. My sister and I had to toss the coin for dates regarding our own parties.

The most moving experience at Hickory Sticks was a Holy Baptism. The families living on my in-laws place asked if a baptism would be possible on Palm Sunday afternoon. With the congregation dressed in white singing familiar gospel songs, preaching which was heard in heaven, and candidates who were unsure of this meaningful act. This memorable occasion has never been forgotten.

Daddy was very "inclusive" and his membership cards read: "is entitled to fishing if in good standing."

When Hickory Sticks was officially dedicated on land loaned to him from God, a poem was written by a happy guest.

"On a hilltop high neath the wide blue sky stands a cottage, cozy and neat, with it's latch- string out to folks all about and the welcome rings true and sweet. The pine scented breeze gently rustles the trees, Stirring sounds of the wild bird call. There, your cares fade away, as your soul seems to pray, And you feel God's peace over all."

Enjoy!

HIGH SCHOOL FRIENDS

Remember when we were in high school? I loved every minute of it except geometry in Ann E. Brown's room and getting stung by a bee in L.B. Smith Science room where he raised bees.

The main reason I loved high school is explained in one word – friends. My longest local friendships from Kindergarten, Lila, Nena, Frank, and Minette graduated with me twelve years later. It was during our most formative years, 14-18, that made an impression. We looked up to the upper classmen as they were leaders in our "educational city". As years progressed we were looked up to as leaders, matured by experience through our studies and school responsibilities. From 8-3 we were guided in our behavior, studies, and expectations. Granted the faculty earned a lot of credit, but our peers challenged us as well.

Reflecting on opportunities available were a variety of organizations. Scholastic clubs, Musical, Historical, Languages, Journalism, ROTC, Athletics all composed of students/friends learning order, organizational skills, Roberts Rules of Order and fellowship. We got a taste of special interests and usually found our niche "in the city" and perhaps in life. Assisting us in choices were faculties providing guidance, encouragement, and availability from 7:30 until --! Every student regardless of grades had this exposure, a matter of choice.

As students on that first day of the eighth grade at Byrd and Fair Park we consolidated into a student body and eventually life long friends. I'm touched when I read the obituaries mentioning being a graduate of one of our high schools. Going to lunch with my friends of 1950 it's a joy to see Mable '33 and Carolyn '33 still having fun.

All this comes down to a Homecoming celebrities.

Reviewing Byrd's mission statement I'm sure Fair Park and Captain Shreve share in its definitions. It states "to establish among the diverse student population a strong foundation for lifelong learning by nurturing, guiding and challenging its students to achieve their maximum potential!"

This was proven when Captain Shreve honored its 2008 Circle of Honor recipients: Loretta Geneux, Senator Lydia Jackson, Dr. Patricia Kitchen, Ben Marshall and Lillian Michiels.

October 10th Byrd's Alumni Hall of Fame honors Robert Crosby, Gwen Talbot Hodges, Tom Parker, Patricia Peyton, Bob Scivally, and former teacher Barbara Whitehead.

On October 17th Fair Park will celebrate the school's 80th year that's 1928! Also present will be members of 1952 celebrating their only state football championship.

Just think this is only a minute list of graduates representing the "can-do" attitude of each school. Our lists include generals, judges, scientists, authors, educators, athletes, doctors, legislators, musicians, and many, many more!

Byrd's Alma Mater written by Dorothy Helm Welbourne applies to Any school's graduate. "Byrd we stand to honor thee, alma mater true, loyal homage we will bring through the years to you. Loyalty, honesty with our friendship hold, always deep written our hearts the purple and the gold". Matt – I'm sorry!

HOLIDAYS AND GRANDPARENTS

Remember when we were little boys and girls and we wondered where we would be having Thanksgiving and Christmas dinners? Both occasions demanded that we be with family members, in-laws, out-laws, and kissing cousins. We didn't have to check DNA because if Grandmother had red hair nine-tenths of her offsprings had red hair – no questions asked.

So the proof was there as far as family went, but where was the destination? Grandparents usually hosted until old age, bad eyesight, mileage or they said, "We're sick and tired of having to clean up after zillions of relatives even though everyone took home leftovers!" Tom Brokaw described our parents correctly as the "greatest generation", and as Daddy would say, "He hit the nail on the head". My interpretation is those wonderful people were raised on leftovers, wore hand-me-downs, and walked 10 miles to school in the snow – and then won the war. What heroes! Today children are at a disadvantage. With "take out food", inexpensive clothes, and school bus delivery from home to school all they have to do is chew, point, and open the door -- what a life! The older we became the more we ventured out to friends, school, and church. Our world seemed completely controlled by our parents which took the pressure off of us.

Our neighborhood was that world which housed us, fed us, educated us, and sustained us in numerous ways. The big break/crack came when we started to grade school and met others, younger and older, from adjacent neighborhoods and our world grew profoundly.

Neighborhoods in Shreveport, today they are subdivisions, had names chosen by the developers. "Sunny Slope" is where I hail from. I haven't the vaguest idea of its origin except it was the Will Fullilove's property. Broadmoor was developed by A.C. Steere whose family vacationed at the Broadmoor Hotel in Colorado.

In high school my new friends came from North Highlands, Barksdale, and Highway I who rode the school buses. Cedar Grove, Highland, South Highland, and the downtown area brought me more. In 1945 (?) all Shreveport grade schools were divided between Byrd and Fair Park, and my world become larger with 2000 students.

By graduation Shreveport was steadily growing since the war. We could drive and venture out of our own "environmental womb". Leaving our neighborhoods to visit friends, skating rinks, picture shows, the lakes, churches, and schools gave us confidence in preparing for the "big one" –earth!

Over the years we've become a little "nomadic". Webster defines it as "roaming about from place to place, aimlessly, frequently, or without a fixed pattern of movement". We usually knew why and where we were going – and as a teenager I'd better be back home on time!

As young adults we've matured enough to know that our parents were smarter than we were. Now we're able to seek and implement any advice given. With college degrees, new jobs, weddings to people out of neighborhood, out of state, and out of mind! Oh – oh – we'd didn't think about where we would spend Thanksgiving/Christmas when we traveled the "center aisle". Now the fun begins!

Orvis tells me he took his young family back to Missouri every Christmas regardless of where his job was. Thank goodness his wife Doris was from the same neighborhood! Traveling with five people, their suitcases, presents, etc., etc., etc. was always a memorable experience – says he.

So here we are at holiday time again. Things change but somehow they always stay the same. I wouldn't have it any other way. NOT aimlessly and NOT without a fixed pattern of movement- we know we'll be with those whom we love and those who love us.

Mr. Rogers knew what he was talking about.

IMAGINATIONS

I'm having such fun "remembering when" with friends, family, and strangers by letters, phone calls, and stops along my daily routes. Seems like a big game with no rules or regulations. One article will remind us of another and then another! They are accompanied with every emotion possible – laughter, lumps in throats, smiles, memories, embarrassment, and tears. I'm so glad I live in Shreveport because the opportunity of seeing friends and acquaintances of the past years is most enjoyable.

As I recall we never planned anything in the summer – it just happened. We definitely went to Sunday school and church and to each others Vacation Bible Schools (we were very ecumenical). Life in Sunny Scope subdivision was an impromptu way of living, and it worked.

"Our play" had no beginning, no end; it could take place anywhere, no winners/losers, no boundaries. "Our play" was only visible in our heads and hearts and "its" name is IMAGINATION. Where would we be without it?

My reason for mentioning this is that I noticed a Times Gannett article recently which made me laugh out loud. Titled "Make Believe Play Vital to Children" by Nanci Hellnich. She writes "Make-believe is more than child's play. It's crucial to the development of creativity, empathy, learning, and problem solving, but it's being squeezed out of children's lives by their commercial world" Hello? Take time to laugh before continuing to read! Am I right in explaining that chefs, inventors, scientists, artists, authors… all started out with an imaginary idea or dream which had its birth in someone's head and heart? This is not new!

I believe my first imaginary initiation was the tooth fairy. Daddy convinced me "she" lived under the bed in the springs (one reason not to bounce on the bed!) and listened to our prayers and parental instructions as to where the pulled tooth should be placed under the pillow to assure a monetary gift. I followed those orders perfectly and was rewarded each time.

Another bedroom experience was the "boogie man". I never had trouble with him because my dog kept him away.

Have you ever locked the door and said "Tick-a-lock"—better safe than sorry with one of those.

Every little girl had a doll, dolls, or paper dolls who could not walk, talk, run, cry, eat, smile, or laugh. But my dolls could do all of those things. All I needed was time, and I could take them anywhere, do anything, anytime, for any reason, by myself or with anyone! It's referred to as "play like" or as we shortened it to "plike". I/we would find a suitable place inside or out, be at a picnic, on a boat, in an airplane, or just on top of the world with our friends and families.

Have you ever lain on a grassy hill and looked up to see a horse formed by clouds but your friend sees a Christmas tree? It's all in the eye of the beholder.

The biggest and best "plike" in history whether boy or girl was Cowboys and Indians. Personally I rode every kind of horse I heard, read about or saw in a picture show. I killed a few cowboys on the trail but my friends traded being the good Cowboys or the bad Indians. With my black pigtails I was always a "squaw who rode a fast horse and used a pistol and a bow and arrow".

My friend Webster's reply to what is imagination: "the act or power of forming a mental image of something not present to the senses or never before wholly perceived in reality". It's not a crime to imagine, because I think we are rich with ideas that no one else has ever thought of – it's a talent each of us has to make us original and one of a kind.

There's one sacred location which holds more imagination thought possible—the library. Books abound with words, but we supply the visual image. Desires, dreams, illusions, -- its all there waiting for you. Get a card, find a comfortable chair there or at home, turn your imagination button on and enjoy …!

KINDERGARTEN BROKE MOTHER'S APRON STRINGS

Remember when you were told to stop daydreaming and get to work? Well, here I sit at my dining room table after having cleared it of the Christmas decoration. I like to write my stories here because of the trees outside, my busy street, and familiar walkers. We've been here 37 years and for the past 10 years a gentleman runner passes with his dog at 10:30. The next day I was sweeping leaves off of the porch when he came at 11:15! I told him he was late and he promised to do better and he did the next day – at 10:30. It takes a village!

Our company has just left after enjoying 5 days with us. With 4 daughters, 2 of his, 2 of mine we have 2 sons-in-law, 11 grandchildren including spouses, and 7 great-grandchildren! That's 26 and thank goodness they didn't come at once. We've had one reunion, and it was fun.

Reflecting on who I saw, where we went, and delicious food eaten, my Christmas really pressed home when we attended St. Marks Christmas Eve Services. The most pleasant observation was the number of families with children and grandchildren who live out-of-town but gather for our holiday.

I arrived early and found an old friend from kindergarten saving seats for her family. I was early so I sat down with Minette Defrance Haynes, as pretty as ever. Naturally we began the "remember when" games amid giggles.

In 1937 we started to Mrs. Nell Kilgores' kindergarten who with her sister Mrs. Johnette Kirby, were A.C.Steere's sisters. He built each of them beautiful homes on Kings Highway across from the Shrine Hospital. With each house having a huge front porch it made a perfect place to take our picture, which we each still have. I reminded her I was standing on the back row between Fred Meadows and Frank Green, who was my boyfriend. She bristled a bit when she explained, "He was my boyfriend!" We both still love him. Of the 26 in our class, 18 that I know of are still living! And of those, 13 came to our 50th High school reunion! We must have done something right!

Kindergarten was so special. Miss Cherry played the piano and we were taught the minuet, listened to classical music. Monkey bars and swing set were huge! We learned to play together, be responsible, and if you made a mess <u>you</u> cleaned it up!

At Christmas we made clay handprints for our parent's presents. After they were fired we wrapped them and proudly presented them. Daddy, who loved to tease me, tapped me on my head and broke mine into a million pieces! I cried until "next year" and so did Daddy.

Julie Watson Bishop's father was the manager of Dairyland Milk Company. Our picture had us lined up on the curb under the Dairyland sign. Lila Scott Mills and I are on opposite ends with her seeing if I'm behaving- she still does!

Not only did we attend kindergarten together but some joined me at Barret for 7 years, Byrd for 5 years with some at Centenary with me. My good friends Nena Courtney Flournoy and Lila declare we stick together because we know too much about each other.

In these two pictures we are in sweet little dresses, smocked, ruffled, beautiful collars, Mary Jane shoes, and white sox. The boys are wearing sailor collared shirts and short pants. It's half and half with oversized bows and berets. Nena and Toinette Sloan Jacobs' bows could have lifted them up on a windy day! Mother saved my big ones for Sundays- go figure.

The best part of kindergarten was that I lived around the corner so I had the pleasure of visiting these women all the time until they moved.

Since kindergarten was not involved in the public school system then and even when my children were small I consider it a privilege to have attended one. It's the first break with apron strings - which whether we like it or not - has to be done. We've all come a long way since age 5, our first year of independence. How fun to remember and you never know who you'll run in to - Jim Haynes went to Mrs. Kilgore's who prepared him for Minette!

I know each of you has a story on stories to share. Let me hear from you.
byrdyjo@aol.com

LEARNING VALUABLE LESSONS

Dear Readers, I used to pretend a friend, Clement Clark Moore, wrote me this letter of his experience on Christmas Eve when we were both children. Read every word and remember.

"T'was the night before Christmas and all through the house, not a creature, was stirring not even a mouse! The stockings were hung by the chimney with care in hopes that St. Nicholas soon would be there. The children were nestled all snug in their beds while visions of sugar-plums danced in their heads, and mamma in her kerchief, and I in my cap had just settled down for a long winter's nap.

When out on the lawn there arose such a clatter, I sprang from my bed to see what was the matter? Away to the window I flew like a flash, tore open the shutters and threw up the sash. The moon on the breast of the new-fallen snow gave a luster of midday to objects below. When what to my wondering eyes should appear but a miniature sleigh and eight tiny reindeer. With a little old driver so lively and quick I knew in a moment it must be Saint Nick!

More rapid than eagles his coursers they came, and he whistled (like me) and shouted and called them by name: "Now, Dasher! Now, Dancer! Now, Prancer and Vixen! On Comet! On Cupid! On Donder and Blitzen! To the top of the porch, to the top of the wall! Now dash away, dash away, dash away all! As dry leaves that before the wild hurricane fly, when they meet with an obstacle, mount to the sky. So up to the house – top the coursers they flew, with the sleigh full of toys – and St. Nicholas, too. And then in a twinkling I heard on the roof, the pouncing and pawing of each little hoof, as I drew in my head and was turning around down the chimney St. Nicholas came with a bound.

He was dressed all in fur from his head to his foot, and his clothes were all tarnished with ashes and soot. A bundle of toys he had flung on his back and he looked like a peddler just opening his pack. His eyes how they twinkled! His dimples how merry! His cheeks were like roses, his nose like a cherry. His droll little mouth was drawn up like a bow, and the beard on his chin was as white as the snow. The stump of a pipe he held tight in his teeth, and the smoke it encircled his head like a wreath. He had a broad face and a little round belly that shook when he laughed like a bowl full of jelly. He was chubby and plump - a right jolly old elf, and I laughed when I saw him, in spite of myself. A wink of his eye and a twist of his head soon gave me to know that I had nothing to dread.

He spoke not a word, but went straight to his work, and filled all the stockings; then turned with a jerk and laying his finger aside of his nose; and giving a nod, up the chimney he rose. He sprang to his sleigh to his team gave a whistle; and away they all flew like the down on a thistle. But I heard him exclaim, ere he drove out of sight: "Happy Christmas to all, and to all a good night!"

Santa left with a smile on his face, an empty bag, a team of reindeer to return to the North Pole. The Kings and Santa invented the art of Christmas giving. But it's a two-way street – learning to be a gracious giver AND a gracious receiver. It's always the thought that counts.

The Christian year begins December 25 of every year. Teddy Allen's December 14th article relates "Bethlehem tells us that the loveliness of life is not in possessions, it is in our relationships".

As children it's all about ME. As adults lessons are learned and it's all about Faith, Family, Truth, Love, Responsibilities, and Understanding. We hear "the story" as we live "our story"; beginnings, endings, additions, subtractions, surroundings, smiles, sadness, and Holy Celebration.

Happy Hannukkah and Merry Christmas!

LOSING LOVED ONE

We probably don't realize it, but I'd be willing to bet we say "Remember when" several times a week. It's not that we are challenging each other's memory concerning something special – it's bringing that person, place, thing, front and center which might have been deeply embedded in our hearts and minds. (These two organs (I believe) are part of the same big organ because of the emotional hook-up.) These events are imprinted for life with no eraser.

Your mind lives your experiences, and they are sent immediately to your storage bin/heart. From time to time they surface and afford us an opportunity to re-live, re-laugh, and re-love. There's nothing like having that first baby, grandchild, or great-grandchild; being with friends and laughing about times spent at different ages of your life; walking down the aisle "into the eyes" of your loving spouse to be; but most of all flipping through those pages in your memory "space" at any given moment which involve every possible emotion!

Several years ago Sally Fields starred in the movie "Places in the Heart", one of my all-time favorites. It's a very poignant story of hardship, decisions, and determination – in other words life itself filling those "places".

As I've related before – I loved school, everything about it except four teachers in sixteen years. One of the biggest "places" in my heart is filled with those wonderful men and women who tried to teach me.

My first favorite was Annie Merrill Graham Scarborough. Family and friends gathered last Saturday to honor her as she was finally laid to rest beside Dan, her husband. Our association began in 1940, age 8, at Barret School, as my third grade teacher. Leaving there after several years she taught at Smith Highlands for a zillion years. I don't dare guess how many 8 year olds had that pleasure, but I'm positive each one was convinced he/she was special in her eyes. This was all anyone needed to do better in the three R's! Her minister, children, grandchildren, and friends spoke adoringly with their stories. Remember when?

Another "place" in our hearts is the one for pets, especially dogs. Besides being a warm body, a tail wager, happy to see you, loves attention, eats anything, will "hold it" until you open the door, alarms you when danger approaches, and minds you most of the time—you realize that you're got the perfect marriage. This thing doesn't talk, tell, fuss, get mad, or serve leftovers! A dog is completely trustworthy concerning conversations and secrets and will kiss if he/she believes it is necessary.

You've all been there – dog, cat, gerbil, bird, rabbit whatever – and you remember their names, ages, and species. Until recently our grandog Mollie age 9 and Billy age 8 were constant companions to their owners and family members who will be well remembered. They led fantastic lives amidst their owners' lives, until they peacefully passed from this place to the next. I believe whole heartedly that dogs go to heaven – where else since their DOG spells GOD backwards. We all realize that a pet can be replaced but not that personality – those big beautiful eyes – on that long tongue waiting to kiss.

And our ages Orvis and I make sure we read the obituaries daily. Not a week goes by that we don't lose a friend or acquaintance. But do we realize how many other lives and organizations are touched by that one loss such as friend Linda. She shared an interest in about every supporting group of the arts in Shreveport. It would behoove us to take the baton which fell from her hand and continue to encourage others in helping to improve our city, that would be her wish. MY friends' "place" is getting too full!

November 1 and 2, All Saints' Day and All Souls' Day respectively, are "Christian feasts in honor of and a day of prayer for faithfully departed souls". You know who they are in YOUR "place". God Bless Us All.

MOTHERS INFLUENCE

Remember when your mother was your MOTHER? I was completely brainwashed by her adages and the Golden rule. I loved her and she loved me, raising me to be the best little girl in Shreveport.

Mother's personality as I finally figured it out was a combination of Edith Bunker, Scarlett O'Hara, General McArthur, and Mary, Mother of Jesus. Simply put a sweet naive soul, a beautiful southern lady, a strict disciplinarian and deeply religious woman. Those of you who knew Flora Belle will agree. I loved her to pieces!

Mother's day since 1908 is next Sunday. I'm thrilled for this special day of recognition – not for me but for Mother and my daughters who are Mothers. Recently I read, "There are moments when you are your Mother and your daughter at the same time." That's scary.

Mother was everything to/for me, a confident, supporter, provider of all my material and spiritual needs, chauffer, bank, and disciplinarian with the help of Daddy and Kiki. We rely on Mothers 24/7 until age 18. That's 6570 days and nights which equals to 157,680 hours. I truly don't understand how she managed to have a life of her own, for family, community, personal and church commitments. It was a miracle.

Remember your questions, what can I do today, why can't I have that, why can't I go? Then came the cry's for help, I'm going to tell my Mother on you, I fell down and I'm bleeding, she hit me, Anne's been crying and I don't know why? The list goes on.

Just think how fortunate we are to <u>have</u> Mothers, <u>be</u> Mothers and hopefully grandmothers to be connected to our history and gender. We must as Mothers, be the source so that we live in our Children's hearts forever. It's such a special gift to treasure memories of times spent with them. Then they are blessed with children and the process begins again.

When that famous cord is cut we are separated from our Mothers only by space, but you are left with a belly button as a reminder of her. Check it out today. The growing up process never ceases, its fun today and a mountain to climb tomorrow, but we survive.

The tragedy in this process is when we age. Illness, dependency, loss of loved ones- all monumental. The nursing home adventure was almost more than I could endure. Mother died of natural causes after 7 ½ years. With my family and friend's love, help and guidance I survived and wrote a journal to pass on to my children and friends. No bad stuff just memories.

One day Mother and I were visiting when she said, "I'm having such a good time I wish Joanne was with us." Another day she phoned me a dozen times. That afternoon I reprimanded her. As she looked up form her wheelchair she exclaimed, I'm so sorry I disappointed you, MOMMA!" This was something THIS Mother couldn't fix. Later a friend explained that we are children until we lose our parents – I was on my way to growing up.

Liz and Anne are such good mothers. Liz's Connor is 16, Anne's Christen is 25 and Scott is 23. They are perfect grandchildren (as all grandchildren are!) I love seeing a little bit of me emerge in the way they are raising their children, and at times my mother sneaks in. So different yet alike.

Mother loved flowers and raised roses, hydrangeas, azaleas, camellias, Easter lilies and a sweet-heart rose which is 70 years old in my yard. Mother flowered neighbors, hospital rooms, meetings, and Kings Highway Christian Church. Seemingly this talent skipped a generation because Liz and Anne caught the flower gene.

Mother was at home at 3:00, called everyone Dahlin', always wore a dress until she was 70 and bought a pantsuit!

Remembering the way she walked, answered the phone, whistled me home, fussing at me before we broke into laughter, hugging, the smell of Evening in Paris, and that goodnight kiss from birth until forever – priceless!

Mother's last words were, "I'm going, Joanne" – still sharing plans for the day. I loved her so much – Happy Mother's Day to all Mothers.

MUSIC AND FRIENDS

Remember the first organized music we were expected to appreciate? It was the rhythm band in kindergarten for me. I was appointed as the triangle player. I only remember "Twinkle, Twinkle, Little Star" when I played furiously every time the word <u>twinkle</u> was sung!

Mother sang "Lullaby and goodnight" to me and I to my dolls. Then there was "Where oh where has my little dog gone, oh where oh where can he be?" On Sundays we sang "Jesus Loves Me." "It's your stand-by when things get muddled," advised my wonderful friend Nell Ray. We're never too old for that kind of musical encouragement.

"Itsy Bitsy Spider," "Mary had a Little Lamb" and "Three Blind Mice" completed our repertoire. With dogs, spiders, mice, lambs – it's a wonder we didn't have bad dreams. Being the well-adjusted children that we were while singing about animals, helping to win the war in dozens of ways, going to school and minding the Victory Garden – who had time to dream?

It's difficult to imagine the person who wrote "mares eat oats and does eat oats and little lambs eat ivy." Try saying that 10 times and that's the title of #1 on the Hit Parade! Or the three little fishes who swam over the dam? "Boop, Boop, diddle and a wadum chew (?)" All these produced by an enlightened civilization? On occasion one's taste in music is compared to one's hair length – you decide that yourself!

But the <u>music</u> – my how times change! Webster says: Music: the science or act of ordering tones or sounds in succession, in combination, and in temporal relationships to produce a composition having a unity and continuity. I knew that!

In reality, music is our gift. It can be loud/soft, fast/slow, sung/played, one instrument/a 500 member marching band, love/death, there's something for everyone – it is referred to as the universal language.

My cherished friend Dottie and I met in the Centenary Choir, she was the accompanist. Having very limited musical knowledge I had no idea of the love, dedication, and absorbing quality which completely captivated her soul, mind, heart, and body.

As we sat listening to the Wideman finalists last year I finally learned to musically appreciate my old friend. Her body was there, but the rest of her was housed in 5 lines full of notes – be they sharps or flats, pianissimo, or forte, read or memorized. She later explained that she is consumed with music and could not live without it. I'm sure Dottie and Don our organist are in sync as to the musical influences on them. Everything in their thinking is translated into a musical connotation, a mood cushion which can alter any emotion.

My cellist friend Ruth becomes a part of her instrument (in my eyes) during the Symphony concerts. Watching her I can almost hear HER strings above all the others because of the boldness and steadiness of her bow held by a loving hand. Pressing the correct strings with her fingers that cello sings with eloquent strength.

Music is one of our most precious gifts of life. The opportunity of hearing a familiar melody washes waves of emotion over us which we hold dear in our hearts. Being able to re-live precious moments with people, places, and things is a privilege and a joy.

Chopin's Etude in E Major with words by Roy Ringwold follows as "A Hymn to Music." Cheesy Voran chose it as the signature theme for the Centenary College Choir.

"O sacred art, o music fair with radiant sound dispel the darkening cloud of fear and care. Speak to us thy universal language of love and of prayer. Melt into tears the icy heart, bring out forgiveness from the stony mouth, and join angry hands. Teach us how to gain from thee the lessor of thy harmony, how wild diversities of sound combine so may we turn from discard and learn peace in thy design.

Holy song, o song of love, inspire our hope, illumine our desire, restore our faith. May we recognize in thee a symbol of eternity a prelude to the mightiest song of all. So must we sing ever answering thy beloved call, o sacred art, o music fair, our thanks to thee."

May the Shreveport Symphony et al harmonize for many years to come.

MY SECOND MOTHER

Remember when we memorized dates in American History? It's because history is our best teacher of what works and doesn't work. The War of 1812 is probably the only date which the "politically correct" can't change. Webster's definition of politically correct originated in 1990 and defined as "conformity to a belief that language and practices which could offend political sensibilities should be eliminated. Understand?

Here is my family history as witnessed with our own eyes, ears, and hearts, a time which was very exceptional. As each February returns I am reminded of Black History month. I pay tribute to a special person in my life.

Being born in 1932 was not a happy time in America. The depression caused citizens to lose businesses, jobs, families, homes, and lives. Luckily Daddy's was secure. Sharing this period of history, you will appreciate my story. Educate your kin about your history.

Lillie Mae Burnham, an 18 year old Negro woman needed a job badly. Daddy hired her 3 months before I was born as a "maid." Webster's defines maid as "a young woman hired for domestic work." When she walked into our home she became one of our family. It wasn't what she did for "us" but what we all did for each other. She was a member in the truest sense forever! We were not wealthy to have a maid – people needed jobs and Kiki's job was with us! In order that she not look like other neighborhood maids, mother the seamstress made her blue dresses which she wore with pride.

Lillie became Kiki by me and quickly adapted to the Sherrods. With Mother she was a companion, friend with whom she shared the good and bad times, and co-parent of my sister and me. They canned vegetables and fruit preserves during the war, combed my long black curls together, divided decision – making when I misbehaved! She never had children therefore Mother approved of sharing me. Kiki's social life included dances on the Roof of Calanthean Temple. Mother made her evening dresses, and next day we heard songs and danced together.

For Daddy Kiki filled several roles. Being highly organized she kept our meals on schedule for business trips, ironed his white shirts to perfection, took messages and kept me quiet when he was sick. Required to have bed rest for 6 months Daddy had been very active but developed leg cramps. He credited Kiki for saving his sanity and suffering by leg massages daily.

As for me Kiki was my first best friend, playmate, teacher, discipliner and second mother. We understood each other perfectly. I rode on her back when she vacuumed, I cried when she sang because the Spirituals were beautiful, taught me that a friend-boy was just a friend but a boy – friend wanted a date, then rocked me in mother's rocker til Byrd's graduation! What a life!! She also convinced me I was helping her clean my room and her one failure was not teaching me to iron (because she was a perfectionist).

Several years ago Mother and Kiki were taken to Schumpert's ER. I introduced myself as Mrs. Sherrod's daughter on Monday. On Tuesday Kiki was there with a broken wrist. After using the same identification and explaining the lack of blood lines the nurse asked "how many mothers I had?" One of each.

Eventually Kiki wanted more. She had always wanted to go to Beauty School so Daddy paid for that and set up shop in her home. She was proud.

My friends had 2 mothers also Lila's Tavie, Banny's Samantha, Anne/Liz's Bessie, Mabel's Aunt Baby and Connor's Laverne.

I've been blessed with these two women of different colors on the outside, but the color of love for me on the inside. They are always with me.

At Kiki's funeral her friend asked me, "Are you Lillie's "white baby Joanne"? I felt so honored and loved to be remembered that way. My eulogy was read, songs and scripture were dedicated to a wonderful Christian woman well on her way to heaven.

Lillie Mae Burnham shared all important events in my life, but I was privileged to share her life. I am so indebted to my "3" very precious parents – yesterday, today, and tomorrow! I owe them my life.

PLAYGROUND TEAMWORK

Remember when we were in grade school and looked forward to the only "no school days" between January 1 and May 31? They were Good Friday which was on our calendars and Field Day which was when Barret's principal Miss Bartoff declared it to be! She probably checked the Farmer's Almanac because it never rained on our field day. Plans were made by teachers concerning team and individual sports.

Barret occupied ½ city block whose front door faced Barret Street and the back door of Barret Place on Fairfield. Between the two was ½ block of land which the Barrets donated to the school. Thankfully the city closed Barret Street for easy access to our new playground.

Passing a school's field day recently I noticed matching t-shirts, $100 tennis shoes-you get the picture. At our field day we finally got to wear shorts! We wore our old school shoes because we didn't have a coupon for playshoes!

Team sports I remember were softball, tug-of-war, Dodgeball, and Red Rover. The bad part of team sports was dividing the class in half. One of my teachers did it perfectly! She picked two captains who quickly chose the "best" players. For the next team sport the last one chosen before became the captain of the new team. New "problem" – everyone wanted to be chosen last!

Since Peggy and I played with neighborhood boys our softball skills were recognized quickly. Called strikes and balls were omitted which meant you hit the ball or struck out. Teachers sat in chairs on either side adorned in their teaching dresses, hose, heels, and big straw hats while keeping score. How did they do that?

Dodgeball was a circle of one team's members surrounding the other team who "dodged the ball" being thrown to hit and make them step out of the circle. Did we keep score? Beats me – but my bruises hurt!

Tug-of-war was fun because a mud puddle was dug, filled with water and challenged one team to drag the other team through it. Played by 6th and 7th graders this tug could get personal!

Red Rover Red Rover let Lila come over!! Each team grasped each others hands/forearms as an opposing team member would run as fast as possible trying to break their grip. If he/she did she went back "home!" After a few attempts you ended up with a stomach ache on an attack of appendicitis!! This was fun?

My favorite individual sport was jump rope although Sarah, Bobbie, Susie, Cooper, and Sue were all good. Realizing that's all we had to do at recess besides Dodgeball it was the safest. We jumped with a single rope – alone or with someone while reciting a verse. "Cinderella dressed in yellow went upstairs to see her fellow. Made a mistake and kissed a snake." Disgusting!
Double Dutch was jumped using two ropes swung in opposite directions. I could get in, but couldn't get out!

With long legs the relays were where I excelled. My love of running came in handy when playing football with neighborhood boys. Come to think of it, was I running away or chasing them? Regardless – I won a few ribbons.

Three-legged races were fun. Advice: don't partner with a left-handed friend because they are also left-footed – no ribbons there!

Considering the physical abilities and endurance involved with these activities, the school yard was where we first learned to play as a team. Having observed team spirits through the war efforts, this was different. Obviously our parents, teachers, and peers were watching and judging our actions. We learned to be fair, loyal, and strong for our team in order to be winners. Thankfully by the 6th and 7th grades we discovered the importance of teamwork.

By the end of Field Day we were ready for a treat. Costing a nickel were Eskimo Pies, popsicles, and Dixie cup iced cream with movie star pictures on the tops. Uncle Joe's Bottling Company on Southern Avenue provided Red Rock Colas, and Mrs. Ravenna's Oatmeal cookies from the cafeteria cost 2¢.

When I think about all we did as children, I wonder how many hours we had in a day – must have been a hundred!

POLICEMEN AND FIREMEN ARE MODELS

Remember when your grade school principal called an assembly? At Barret that meant a lot of excitement. A special one on safety occurred each September—and we could hardly wait! Miss Bartoff was explicit concerning the safety of her first thru seventh graders, while they were in her care. After 3 o'clock she expected them to practice what they had learned at school.

As a hint of what that assembly concerned we could hear a loud motorcycle approaching our school which I'm sure was heard from Southern to Fairfield. From the other direction came a red car with a siren on full blast. Settling down in the auditorium, we sat motionless until the curtain opened exposing two uniformed giants! With our breath taken away we sat spellbound with eyes and mouths wide open.

When the policeman stepped forward we visualized his motorcycle which most law men rode. He was dressed in black boots, wide leather belt, pistol in its scabbard, helmet, and a saucer sized badge pinned to his white shirt. I would have confessed to any crime of the day! I'm sure some of the "bad boys" attending were having second thoughts of their future actions. The officer's topic centered on our safety – crossing streets with traffic lights and not to play in them, bicycle rules, walking with or without sidewalks, and courtesy in our mobility in the future.

As school children we were accustomed to seeing two types of policemen. Our first encounter with the law was the school crossing guards who were retired policemen – bored but still woke up at 6:00. With this job they worked the crossing, went home, took a nap, back at noon to the crossing, home for dinner and a nap, back to the 3:00 crossing and home. All this work was rewarded monetarily plus hugs, smiles, holding hands of first graders, cookies from thankful parents and an assortment of good and bad weather. If it didn't work out they could quit, but our Johnny at the corner of Southern and Wilkinson commanded that crossing all my Barret years. He knew everyone's name, asked if you were sick yesterday – I missed you, required walking your bicycle across, held your hand if you had on skates, and any questions he thought appropriate.

The motorcycle policeman was held in the highest regard. This came to my attention the first time I drove our car by myself. Filled with the fear of God, Daddy, and any riding policeman in me I was a cautious driver. When I SAW/SEE a motorcycle behind me I feel guilty – of what?

To prove a point one night Josephine and I were returning from the Strand having seen "Forever Amber" which we were forbidden to see. We thought we could get away with it when out of nowhere a motorcycle appeared with a loud siren. We were scared to death and wondered how our mothers managed to involve the law to arrest us for seeing "Forever Amber"!

Much to our relief we were advised that Josephine had forgotten to turn the headlights on. That was 1948 and I still think about headlights except to my satisfaction they are automatic in 2008!

The other giant stepped forward covered completely by his helmet, huge boots, long overcoat, and carrying a piece of hose attached to a 24(?) inch nozzle. He lectured compassionately to his young audience – don't play with matches, wall outlets, be careful burning leaves while roasting marsh mellows, firecrackers, and much more. We looked at these champions with deep respect and those they represented.

As second-graders we journeyed to the Line/Wilkinson fire station led by teacher Madelyn Rogers. We sat on the ladder truck, slid down the pole, and pushed the horn and siren. Years later I took 3 year old grandson Scott to visit "my fire station". Standing in owe we heard the loud siren which shocked Scott so much it scared the "you know what" out of him. As a result his "want-to-be" list excluded fireman.

Safety hasn't changed. Cars/bicycles travel the SAME way. Sidewalks are for walkers, baby strollers, dog walking.

Runners face traffic and parking lots require courtesy and eye contact. Otherwise hangup and look both ways!

PUBLIC SERVANTS

Remember when gasoline was 35 cents a gallon plus all the services that were included each time you drove into a filling station? All this was taken care of by the owner/manager plus a young helper. Webster came to mind and defined public service: "the business of supplying a service to any and all members of a community." All of this service is rendered by a public servant: "a servant is one who serves others."

With today's job market I am reminded of my personal list of "public servants" which begins at the corner of Kings Highway and Centenary. Through the years we've all had favorites, but mine is Jim Ashley who operated the Amoco filling station for 45 years. He was a quiet-spoken man with a vast knowledge of cars and everything associated with them. He came with the Orvis package when we married so I learned to abide by all his advice which included type of gas, motor oil, air in tires, a little soap in the windshield spray, anti-freeze, a dependable battery, and a swept floor! Where had he been since MY car ownership life?

Lila's mother was widowed in the 40's and was blessed with Mr. Ashley's friendship and automotive knowledge. Her five children joined the parade to the famous corner for help and service. If the car had a problem he could detect it entering his station and repair with haste and perfection.

The Scott family gathered for Saturday lunch including friends feasting on Tavie's delicious dishes. Often there came a knock at the back door accompanied by an invitation to "sit down Mr. Ashley." He was always welcomed.

When Lila and Owen married they realized it was necessary to go to Ashley's for gas before leaving town. What a sendoff for a honeymoon!

From 1945 – 1990 Jim Ashley served friends, doctors, college presidents and professors, widows, lawyers, and strangers in the same manner: as a gentleman, dedicated business man, father, WWII Veteran , with a quiet disposition and a quick wit. I wish he was still pumping my gas!

Another public servant was Carl, our mailman during WWII, who had attended high school with Mother's brother. L.P. was the baby boy of five children whom Mother adored. With twice a day mail deliveries Mother was always anxious for a letter which was announced by Carl's knock on the door. Kiki prepared iced tea and everyone listened as Mother read for all to enjoy, especially Carl. After 2 years in Europe my uncle returned but we still shared tea with Carl.

If you really want to see a "public servant" at work head over to uptown's Brookshires and watch Bill Marshall in action. His mother Frances and I taught at Linwood Junior High. When Bill was a baby we realized his outgoing personality would serve him well.

Years past and I found him sacking groceries and quickly renewed our friendship and realized he had been in high school with Anne and Liz. "We" all take notice of how our groceries are sacked, and I was satisfied. This is not only my experience but all who enter those magic doors. He is knowledgeable of our lives, Orvis' health, a new car, the weather – everything! He always has a smile, can find anything, provides a basket, loads groceries in the trunks, eggs in customer's hands; never seems tired—a bundle of energy who has been honored as an outstanding Brookshire employee- and quite deserving.

When $5 12-inch subways started selling I bought one for Lila and me to share. A worker with a huge smile asked "is this all for you?" I explained I would be sharing it with Lila in the nursing home. Now I'm greeted with "Hi, Miss Jo, how's your friend in the nursing home?" Heads turn waiting for my answer. Subway is not just for Jarred – it brought Ann, a "public servant", and me together.

Isn't it weird how we interact with people knowing nothing about their lives especially their names? We're been taught to do unto others as we would have them do into us for years—Tell Bill and Ann hello!

RESOLUTIONS MAKE US BETTER

I remember Celia Smiley saying, "Go look it up, Joanne." And that's what I did today. I'm referring to New Year's resolutions. Webster's didn't satisfy me so I opened my Thesaurus and discovered what I needed to make a point, the good stuff we all desire: courage, determination, perseverance, zeal, and intention. With hand on heart, "I swear with determination I will persevere to show courage and zeal to accomplish my intention of keeping my New Year's resolutions. (if made) That's a mouthful – need I say more?

After Black-eyed peas & cornbread, (every household has a different menu) my family including Kiki would make "promises" in good faith. As a child and until I married my resolutions covered all sorts of things which probably were broken before noon on January 2!

As an adult I really don't make too many resolutions if any– aloud anyway! My biggest challenge in life is cooking! I hate to cook — the everyday stuff for the two of us but for a PARTY — let's get busy! Having had Kiki in my life she only taught me the basics, set the table, dry the dishes, and visit with her. Wasn't that what kitchens were for?

Married at 25 I had learned to cook a little, but cooking breakfast at 4:30 for a cotton farmer husband was difficult to say the least. Then moving to the country allowed me to cook at 5:00 – whoopee. Then the steady stream of farmer friends for coffee, dinner at 12:00, and supper from 6:00-9:00! I prayed for Kiki, Mother, even God to come help me.

Before we married Orvis we discussed many important issues, Most importantly I stated — "I don't cook dinner at noon" He agreed and we've lived happily ever after — no resolution there.

Several years later Lila found a sign for my kitchen — "Cooking make you ugly." It had my name on it. My family will verify the sign is correct!

Several of my friends defined their ideas of making resolutions. One says to make them we have to have self discipline and if not we fail. Another exclaimed she never made them because they included those responsibilities we should have been doing but didn't like to do." My favorite reported that "Resolutions represent a new beginning, and we acknowledge that we are not perfect. We know our shortcomings, but want to improve and make a difference in our life and the lives of those we love. Time is so precious."

When we wade through all the trouble of trying/ avoiding / ignoring / or even making New Year's resolutions it's all about doing better. The "first 10 rules" we were given are pretty clear, but the second is exceptional. "Love thy neighbor as thyself" which basically says if YOU aren't happy with yourself how can you relate to others and make them happy?

Mother's favorite advice was, "do unto others as you would have them do unto you." (I once heard a comedian advise his audience, "Do unto others BEFORE they do unto you.") It's a challenge in today's world, but be strong and not tempted.

From Shakespeare's Hamlet I tried to raise my children using Polonias' advice to Laertes. "This above all to thine oneself be true, thou can't's not then be false to any man."

Life's challenges and choices are every day. My favorite hate challenge is "the line" popcorn, bank, grocery, etc. I always pick the wrong one and find it hard to smile thru gritted teeth. It's not that important except when it's popcorn.

Real life stuff is about me — and you; our human relationships, religious, our city, country, and environment. What else is there?

Step back a day and pretend it's Jan 1 and make one blanket resolution with me, the Scout Promise, "On my honor I will do my best to do my duty to God and my country, …to help other people at all times, to keep myself physically strong, mentally awake, and morally straight. A scout is trustworthy loyal, helpful, friendly, courteous, kind, obedient, cheerful, thrifty, brave, clean, and reverent."

I'll try if you will.

SHOES

Remember when we put a lot of thought into what we would wear especially when leaving home? It's not the case today. Oh, for the return of the word vanity to our vocabulary: having or showing undue or excessive pride in one's appearance. If today's designers, mothers, and all females on earth could be bitten just once by the "vanity fly" we wouldn't have to look at body parts which should be covered in civilized and polite society. Don't these females realize that "covered up" is more alluring than exposure? There – I'm off my soapbox – maybe I'm jealous!

Since I've been sharing my thoughts of clothes, I've covered blue jeans to skirts, blouses, cashmere sweaters, evening dresses, belts, hats, scarves, gloves, and flowers. But – the best is yet to come cause you can't do without them. In case you don't have the proper ones for a 7:00 party and it's 2:00 – no problem – go find some – SHOES!

My memory only goes back to the war years. I was 9-13, and we had school shoes and Sunday shoes. Ration stamps limiting us to 2 pairs a year (correct me if wrong). My school shoes were tacky brown lace-ups, but I loved my Sunday black patent leather Mary Janes with white sox. Returning home from church I immediately removed them and applied Vaseline to avoid cracking. By the time it took my feet to outgrow them, they wouldn't have cracked anyway! Regardless, I did what I was told.

When I got a little older I was able to leave the children's shoe department and shop at Bakers, Burts, and Franks for casual shoes. Nancy and Ellen remember the red and blue wooden shoes. A piece of leather joined the heel and sole pieces under your arch acting as a hinge and leather straps over your toes and heel/instep. They were the noisiest footprints ever. Being an active child I only had one pair, but they lasted 2 summers.

My other summer favorites were huaraches made of woven leather which would stretch with wearing. With any easy fix you threw them in a bucket of water for a couple of hours and let them dry in the sun. I'd have a "new" pair in a day. However, after a while they started to smell and away they went.

Then came Penney loafers. To be authentic they had to be purchased from J.C. Penney. As soon as you got home you slide pennies into the fold across the top. Ask me why – I did it because the older girls did. Times haven't changed!

My school shoes I died for were saddle oxfords. In order that you didn't want to leave the impression they were new you had to scuff the white part a bit. Don't ask. Andy told me his favorites were his Spalding saddles with a solid piece of rubber sole. Saddles come in white with black or brown and Orvis' are buckskin with tan saddle. They're for everyone.

I loved going to Dryers and Newstadts to see Art Woodruff, best shoe salesman in town, and especially Phelps. Their x-ray machine would catch the truth about the proper shoe fit.

High heels are fabulous for an outfit and attitude. They can turn a ho-hum dress or suit into a striking look. Add a scarf and lipstick and you are ready for any thing.

Teaching school in 1954 I wore the same high heel/pointed toe shoe being shown now as the latest style – HA! Wedges, thongs, ballet, slings, slip-ons, tennies, and zillions of other styles are made out of ANYTHING! Mitzi declares her matching alligator shoes and purse were to die for – she had arrived.

I really don't know what it is about being addicted to shoes. My Liz has many pairs. Son Connor wanted a new pair of tennis shoes at age 4 but Mother refused. At that moment he opened her closet and counted as far as he was capable, then began at one again! He got new tennis shoes.

Today my tennis playing and active feet are almost 76 but from ankles up I'm still kicking. Call me – let's got shopping! I'll be ready at 10:00.

SLEEPING HABITS AND PLACES

Remember when we had to take afternoon naps? Who benefited more – me, Mother or Kiki ? They can be habit forming but not by me. I told both my husbands if they caught me daytime napping to call the hospital or Osborn's. Mother told me that Kiki sat in her rocking chair beside my baby bed and held my hand until I went to sleep. That link could make anything happen.

Webster defines sleep as "the natural periodic suspension of consciousness during which the powers of the body are restored." I restore my powers in seven and a half hours at night. It varies with everyone, so do what you need, because no one can do without it. Short renewals have been described as 40 winks, catnap, siesta, or my favorite, a blanket drill. These can be experienced in airplanes, churches, theatres, or at home in his chair while listening to me! Children can sleep at football games, parades, in strollers, anywhere and as Lila told me on the top of the back seat of their car at age 4. With 5 children in the family I guess they forgot to count noses before putting them to bed!

One of my favorite "sleeps" was on the Pullman car of the KCS Railroad on our overnight trips to Kansas City. The Pullman porter used his 8 inch key to unlock the upper berth to retrieve linens, pillows, and blankets for both berths. His talent in making them up was unbelievable. Our task was getting undressed while sitting on the bed with about 12 inches overhead. Practice made perfect, because the prize was settling down for the sleeping ride into the black night with the moon and stars traveling with us. Occasionally I heard the bell signals on the roads we crossed – not enough to wake me but just a slight melody to put me back to dreamland. The clickity – click of the wheels on the rails which rested on the thousands of cross ties bought by Daddy was restful and reassuring. If you've EVER spent the night on a Pullman I'm sure you can still enjoy it!

Peggy and I enjoyed sleep-over, as referred to in today's lingo. When we were 10 & 12 we decided to sleep outside. Having no tent we constructed our own. We stretched a rope between our badminton posts and hung white sheets with clothes pins forming a big Tepee. Sleeping on army cots we finally slipped into a wonderful night's sleep. When we awoke the next morning we discovered something horrible had happened to our "home." The dew had fallen and so had the sheets which were wet and hanging about 10 inches above our noses. Learn something new every day at that age.

Sleeping habits through the years have been very interesting and original. Mother related how her family of seven slept in the summer BAC (before air-conditioning). She shared a bed with her older sister who was over-weight. As soon as possible she made herself a "Baptist Pallet" on the floor to keep cool and stretch out. My source says the pallet's origin was perhaps after Sunday dinner, with a house full of company it was expected that everyone take a nap. After all necessity is the mother of invention.

When summer came I slept on the screened-porch which was protected from rain on two sides by canvas awnings. In good weather with my bed next to the screen I could look up to the sky and see the moon and thousands of stars while picking out the Big and Little Dipper. Going to sleep in a safe place while smelling, listening, and watching the lightening was magical. I just hoped the sun would shine tomorrow.

After a wonderful summer day with my friends and family, and 3 good meals cooked by Kiki I got my second bath for the day and ran to the porch for a night's sleep. Electric lights out – God's light on, while I recited out loud, "now I lay me down to sleep. I pray thee Lord my soul to keep. If I should die before I wake, I pray thee Lord my soul to take."

Amen.

SONGS THAT LAST

Remember when you heard one of those intellectual ditties sung on radio about how you should use "Prell Shampoo, a little dab will do you? Sometimes you can't get rid of them as I have just proven!

Last week I tried to explain about music, but fell short. It's just so indescribable with notes connected together making it so tranquilizing to our hearts, minds, and souls.

Then someone composes the music _and_ writes lyrics! And we are compromised with another element to love and appreciate. Songs learned early are practically never forgotten as I mentioned about dogs, spiders, mice, and lambs. Those just got us started. The older we became, the themes had more meaning, eloquence, and significance, all of which touched our young hearts at that moment.

Our first memorized songs originated on Sundays – Onward Christian Soldiers. I'll bet you can't recite the first verse but you CAN sing it. Other church related songs were at Thanksgiving – God of Our Fathers (hear those trumpets?) and weddings. In the 30's and 40's did they always have to sing "I Love You Truly" and "Because"?

Then we grew up listening to "Big Band" music which started in 1926 and peaked in the late 30's and into the 50's. These bands were made up of true musicians playing a multitude of songs each having verse and chorus on several instruments.

Orvis explained that these bands began on one coast and travel cross-country on "Route 66" which became a song. In Springfield, MO Orvis was sure he had a date in order to dance the night away in the Masonic Lodge where students, young and old people gathered. "Stags convened in the center of the dance floor as couples danced the outskirts. The band accompanied several soloists. Everyone knew the words because they were heard on radio, 78 records, and jukeboxes. I think it was a pleasant way of being brain-washed because I still remember – thankfully! I can't "sing-along" with today's hit parade. Daddy didn't sing, but Mother and Tennessee Ford had fun singing together!

Sue Ford related to me that before she came to Shreveport in 1942 she had the wonderful opportunity to sing and travel with George Towne and several other orchestras around Texas and Louisiana for 2 ½ years. The songs of her day were very poetic, sincere, and thoughtful. "I'll be seeing you in all the old familiar places that this heart of mine embraces all day through," or "At last, my love has come along, my lonely heart is happy – and life is just a song" (Betcha sang instead of reading.) Good grief – with words like these to listen to. – Keep the radio on!

Traveling with an orchestra one night Sue was approached by a guest in the ballroom who requested they play "Deep Purple." The band and Sue consented after which a $100 bill was slipped into her hand – the band played and Sue sang it - nine times! "When the deep purple falls over shady garden walls, and the stars begin to twinkle in the sky. In the midst of a memory you're coming back to me, breathing my name with a sigh." WOW

Track through your years as a teenager having your first crush on a tall good-looking classmate and remember "our song." What about "White Christmas," "Tara," "Shall We Dance," "Stardust," or your own favorites.

Isn't it strange how we borrow songs and words because we think the writer expressed a feeling better than we can? Cyrano de Bergerac fed his words of love to Roxanne through his friend, we don't feel confident to trust ourselves.

What about lessons learned with songs/words? ABC, Do-re-me, 1-2-3 strikes you're out! and "South Pacific" by Rogers and Hammerstein "You've got to be taught to hate and fear!"

Don't we wonder about the writer's situation when penning his songs? Love songs of opposite extremes, "Some Enchanted Evening" and "Gonna Wash that man right out of my hair." – good or bad advice?

Take a moment during your shower, waiting in line, or while you are going to sleep and remember your favorite song in the circle of your life. Who does it remind you of, where were you? The words and music are inseparable, sweet, calming…restful...z...z...z.

STORE DELIVERIES TO OUR HOMES

Remember when the most important commodity in the business world sold in Shreveport was service? I've already made reference to the downtown store owners and their well-schooled employees. In the golden years of my memories, the 40s and 50s, the war was fought and won, and basically Americans were a happy group. We were devoted to our families and surroundings and willing to help each other with no questions asked. We yearned to serve and be the satisfied customer. This applied to every business venture open to the public.

One of my favorites was the milkman driving his horse and "wagon" up the street to bring our milk early in the morning. A "whoa" to the horse, a rattle of glass milk bottles against each other, steps of the milkman as he placed the bottles on our front steps, a click of the reins with an encouraging kissing sound from the milkman – all had a familiar ring to start my day.

Daddy always brought the milk and newspaper into the kitchen where Mother removed the bottle cap and poured the cream off of the top of the milk –cream- no half and half! Pouring that over a bowl of 40% Bran Flakes with a teaspoon of sugar kept me full til dinner (at noon!)

Following closely behind was the ice man. We had an Electrolux refrigerator but Peggy's family still had an ice box which was divided into 2 parts. The upper part housed the ice block and milk bottles with the lower part full of everything else. Considering the different sizes of ice boxes they ordered different pounds of ice. Every customer had a square card placed in the kitchen window designating how much ice they needed that day.

During the day Mother might need a prescription from Glenwood Drug. With Daddy traveling in the car she asked for home delivery which was provided by a man on motorcycle. I'm sure Jimmy Weyman did a tour of home delivery for Weyman's Drugstore between cooking hamburgers and car-hopping.

Frank Ford related a story of a man named Sam Gerderain (probably misspelled) who drove a horse and buggy around South Highlands. He sold fruit and vegetables and called out his collection of produce for that day. Most remembered was "I got a nice alligator pear (avocado) and ponderosa tomatoes!" Can't you just visualize those streets with children asking for an apple and ladies waiting for Sam's wagon to progress? Nothing like home-grown food!

One man on whom Mother depended all year was the one who sharpened her scissors. He came at no specific time of his but Mother knew by her scissors it was time. Since she made our clothes she needed sharp scissors for cutting fabric. She alternated three pairs and dared me to cut anything other than fabric. I still have her favorite pointed pair and each time I use them I swear I can hear, "What are you cutting with my scissors?"

There were several small grocery stores in our area but the one I remember most was Parker's on Line between Linda and Stephenson. It was small in physical appearance, but large in service. Let me explain. With their delivery service the customer might ask the delivery man to: take out the garbage, change a light bulb, help in an emergency, or enter an unlocked backdoor to place refrigerator items properly and re-lock the door.

Delivery customers were a variety of people, rich people whose cooks called in orders, old or house bound, or those who enjoyed the opportunity of not shopping. Naturally the cost went up when they said, "Charge it."

On Saturday husbands of customers or neighborhood men congregated for coffee. With only 2 chairs the group was small and didn't stay too long. Barnes and Noble stole this idea!

Shopping personally you found the butcher cutting meat and bacon to your specifications, fresh produce, and there weren't 12 kinds of canned green beans! Maybe that's why I don't like to cook!

Combining all these specialties into one store is how Pack-a-Sack was born! – but now they're 7-11! My question is, who servicing from 11-7?

SUMMER SICKNESS

Remember when Summer came and we were convinced that we owned it, could do anything, go anywhere, etc.? Running through the back door and into the house was not on that list. If I was called down only once a day it was a miracle. I just liked to get things done quickly.

Last week I was on the go, not looking where I was going (and barefoot) when I stumped my toe on a chair leg. My "support system" had gone to work-out so I screamed Bloody Murder! Thank goodness no one heard me.   Being   uneasy about looking down I finally realized the nail was still attached as it should be. The floor looked comfortable so I sat down and remembered a similar childhood experience when the nail was completely removed. What was I to do? There were important Summer barefoot projects waiting. How long for a nail to grow back, would I be ordered to bed, house arrest, when could I wear shoes especially in the snow (I plan ahead) and would I be a cripple?? My Mothers came to my aid and promised I would survive and walk normally by September 1--- great!

Our 7th grade teacher at Barret, Kathryn Tillery, had made us memorize John Greenleaf Whittier's "The Barefoot Boy". I immediately saw myself as that boy and crawled to my bookcase and found the poem..."Blessings on thee little man barefoot boy with cheeks of tan". Google up Mr. Whittier's poem because it completely describes what we children saw, heard, did and felt in our Summers. "Ah! That thou couldst know the joy, ere it passes, barefoot boy."

Being incapacitated in Summer was a tragedy or maybe God's payback for sins committed during the school year in class or during recess. After all we weren't perfect! and couldn't be for 24 hours a day for 90 days. But sick for one day for us and our Mothers? Sick meant being confined to bed, shades drawn, and behaving ourselves so that our temperature wouldn't rise. Talk about a challenge!

Funny thing about temperature during the school year, we wanted it high using the healing pad or a dip into a cup of hot tea provided that.

I remember Peggy's case of Scarlet Fever which is very contagious and serious. She wasn't allowed out of her bed much less her room.   Since the recuperation period is long Peggy and I got very bored at our respective homes. Being inventive little children, we came up with an ideal way of including Peggy in play. On the lawn just outside her window our friends gathered around a Monopoly

Board. Peggy chose her token and we decided she was to be first and began the game until we realized she was winning. We couldn't accuse her of cheating because WE were throwing her dice, buying her properties, moving her from Illinois to Boardwalk, passing go AND collecting $200. All of a sudden we heard our mothers calling or whistling us home. We weren't bad losers we just got tired! Yeah –

One of the most painful yet not serious was a sore throat. It was the medical treatment that was painful. Sore throats just appeared and I hated admitting to one because Doctor Mother had 2 remedies. The 12 inch swab dipped in mercurochrome which reached down to my navel or gargling with warm salt water which I fully expected to go into my lungs and drown me! Gag—gag. Was she the inventor of the "Kill on Cure" method of medicine? I realized I had to get well in a hurry!

One semi-serious medical happening was so special that we took pride in receiving this badge of honor. At 6 it validated our natural maturity which would remain with us forever. Dr. W.B. Worley delivered my vaccination, the "live cowpox virus to artificially increase immunity to small pox." The scab, etc. remained 2-3 weeks! No swimming, playing in the washtubs or rain was almost unbearable. But I could still dry dishes.

Thanks and appreciation to those devoted scientists with imaginations working to find healing cures for us to depend on!

Find your scar? I'll show you mine if you show me yours!

SUMMERS ARE BUSY TIMES

Remember how hot, sweaty and rainy it was in last Wednesday's article. Shreveport weather hasn't changed – ever! We can have 3 inches of rain on Tuesday afternoon and wake up to Wednesday's 95° and by 12 o'clock the streets and grass are dry as a bone! I guess Global Warming really was invented by GOD!

By then our mothers were more than ready for us to "go out and play!" Let's face it, as bad as it may sound we were all raised on 4 letter words and I'm proud of it because I passed that on to my children: DON'T DO THAT, SHUT THE DOOR, COME HOME, BE GOOD, HAVE FUN. What an education.

Before we left the house the radio brought us wonderful programs, Saturday's starting at 9:00 Hilltop House, Let's Pretend and Green Hornet, were my favorites.

Most mothers did their major grocery shopping on Fridays, but occasionally they missed picking something up. That's where we were put to "child labor". "I need a box or sack of something of great importance so I want you to go to the store for me." The A and P on Southern was about 4 blocks away and I hated going alone -- no one to chat, laugh, or race with. Call Peggy -- let's roll! Then her mother would say "If you're going get me a _____." Arla Jo might see us leaving and catch up with us. Maybe this is how neighborhood gangs get started -- going to the store -- just hope Mother wasn't in a hurry for her needed item because the fountain at Williams Drugstore sounded like a good watering hole for a cherry cake. We always felt the ride was faster and louder if we clothes-pinned cards to the bicycle frame. As the spokes went round and round we made our presence known!

During those long Shreveport Summer days we never had the problem of saying "There's nothing to do." If so we would have been put to bed immediately.

Our highest aim was trying to keep from "dying from the heat." My favorite was going swimming. Peggy and I were sent to town on the trolley to the YMCA which had a wonderful pool in the basement. I know it sounds like torture, and it was until I learned to swim. It had such a chlorine smell to it that you'd do anything the teacher asked. We learned every stroke possible just to get out and smell fresh air.

We finally made it to the Natatorium on Creswell. After riding by it last week it has diminished in size. But the memories of the diving tower watching Martha's dives, the cold showers before and after entering the pool, the rings, slide, rubber bathing cap and Mother's watchful eyes because she was so afraid of water. What fun we had.

    We all had a bare piece of yard where the grass didn't grow probably because of wear and tear from children's knees. It was under a tree for shade and many a marble game was challenged. I still have all my marbles (that's debatable!) even my "Aggie."
    In contrast you had to find a piece of grass-covered yard that was still a little damp – for mumble peg: "a game in which players try to flip a small knife from various positions so that the blade sticks into the ground," says Webster. Wasn't that what knives were for?

    Since our houses were not air-conditioned the windows and doors were always open for easy cross – ventilation. There was no privacy! Hence the need for a simple foreign language -- pig latin or igpay atinlay – once you get the hang of it – it's easy.

    If new houses were being built in your neighborhood discarded lumber was valuable. 2 X 2 boards 4 feet long were magically turned into stilts. Add a triangle piece for a foot-rest and with practiced balance walking was possible. Soapbox cars were a favorite of Tim who raced them against neighbors and usually won. Tree houses were segregated –boys and girls. Daddy helped us and it was wonderful. I could see forever!

    It's said, "Youth is wasted on the young" -- not where I came from!

SUMMERS ARE FOR CHILDREN

Remember when school was out in May? We couldn't wait to start playing where we left off last August.

Peggy and I loved playing in the water – rain! Where are those soft, slow, and "smell – good" summer rains today? If there was no thunder or lightening we hurried to put on our swim suits. If you think Gene Kelly had fun dancing with an umbrella in the rain you should have been with us while riding bicycles, swinging, or climbing a tree. We wanted to be the first ones to feel the raindrops before they watered the grass or Mother's roses. When we tired of all that activity we'd just lie down on the grass, face up, mouths open and have a wonderful drink of water.

When the rains were slow in appearing we found our mother's #3 washtubs, placed them side-by-side in our backyard, filled them with water and jumped in. I can't recall what we played, but it sure cooled us off. When our skin became wrinkled, Kiki made us get out, but not before splashing our resistance!

On days it rained too hard Mother helped me with my "music". With eight glasses of the same size we filled them with different amounts of water, and tapped them with a spoon. Behold – I had a musical instrument. Mother got sick and tired of "Three Blind Mice"! In this case desperation not necessity was the mother of invention, and the sun couldn't show itself soon enough.

Music can also be played by a group of children using coke bottles. Again with different amounts of liquid the sound varies. Just place the bottle opening against your lower lip and blow. Takes a bit of organization but "Three Blind Mice" is possible.

Our screened front porch was a great meeting place for my neighbors. When it was too rainy, messy or hot to go outside to play, Kiki would set the big Emerson isolating fan up while we played all sorts of games.

Dominos was a favorite because when we tired of matching dots in the game we would set the pieces on end forming a line, curve, or circle, tap the first one in line and watch them fall. When I saw the same display 60 years later at Sci-port I was quite impressed with us.

"Tiddley Winks" was a challenge. You could practice alone and then show-off in the next game. A 2 inch deep, 10 X 10 inch box with a hole in the middle housing a glass cup was the playing board, each player had a number of chips which when flipped were suppose to land in the cup for points. Hope someone else remembers this besides Orvis.

Chinese checkers were popular because 4 could play. The "holey" board was divided into colored triangles with matching marbles. Object of the game was to advance across the board to your matching triangle without being jumped and eliminated by other players.

Another rainy day pastime for me was playing with my dolls. My favorites were my collection of storybook dolls, each dressed to represent a character, country, etc. They are porcelain, 5 inches tall with movable arms and legs. My collection is still intact because I only shared them with Anne and Liz with fever of 100° and confined to bed.

Paper dolls were fun and popular. We saw the picture shows and couldn't wait until the paper dolls came out so as not to forget what they wore. We loved "Shirley Temple", "Snow White", "Cinderella", and my favorite "Gone with the Wind"! All these dolls benefited by living in my doll house.

Three months? Not enough time to accommodate the games, adventures, etc., which we looked forward to enjoying. We took our play seriously, learning to share, be a good winner/loser, helping our younger friends and cleaning up after ourselves. We played sunup to sundown, ate lunch at each others' houses, were disciplined by all mothers and obeyed their rules.

All this plus monopoly, yoyos, cards, Bingo, making model airplanes, reading and radio listening- on a rainy summer day in Shreveport!

SUNDAY AFTERNOON ADVENTURES

Remember the lazy Sunday afternoons in the 30's and 40's? I don't know about yours but ours were busy. With ingenuity and inventiveness and a little boredom thrown in we always found something to do. I looked forward to a car ride in the Spring and Fall. The majority of these outings were with all the family – 4 Sherrods. Babysitters were yet to reach their peak, but the car ride was advertised by Daddy as a great adventure. I bought it — hook— line— and sinker! One of my favorites was driving west on Highway 80 entering the Greenwood Road at the Mansfield Road. Just a block away was the Watermelon Garden and Mina Golf Course. Stopping there after our ride was a definite plan which Daddy never forgot.

Our first stop was Rose Hill, a natural lake/pond used for swimming, just outside Greenwood. We stopped and I would take a short dip with the slides, rings, and diving board, which I ignored because I couldn't swim in deep water!

Following 80 we often stopped where purple wisteria bloomed on a fence for a mile. The scent was delightful and provided such beautiful color to barbed wire. Arriving in Marshall we "made the town square", the train station, and returned home for mini-golf and a cold slice of watermelon. A promise is a promise.

Our southern route took us from Kings Highway and Williams to Fairfield where Mother once again would tell me where the Moores, Marstons, Harmons, Ratcliffs, Smithermans, Wheelesses, and many more lived. Thankfully those beautifully structured homes have survived while only two have disappeared.

Driving over to Ockley with houses on one side and cotton fields on the other could really make you think. It's difficult to realize and reflect on how Shreveport has progressed, because here I sit in Broadmoor 3 blocks past Ockley.

Driving down the Harts Island Road was picturesque and calming beside the levee protecting us against flooding. (But that's another story!) We loved seeing the cotton wagons waiting at Webb and Webb's gin and the vast fields of cotton 5 ft tall on either side of the 2 lane highway. What a sight! Little did I know I would be married to the cotton industry— years later.

Some Sundays we'd stay in town, and our first stop was always Fort Humbug. At that time there was only the entrance and winding roads— no hospital, etc. In the far back was a bluff which provided a perfect lookout of the river. You've heard the story — the confederates were there with a reduced number of troops while the union navy was fast approaching. Someone suggested cutting down the trees, charring them and mounting them to look like cannons. The Union navy swallowed the threat and retreated. It's all in the eye of the beholder — hence Humbug!

Our last stop was Barksdale — before the war. With the speed limit 15 MPH we could enjoy the ride through the gate, the middle of the golf course, and down the boulevard while reading the names and ranks on the beautiful look – alike houses. Then to the flight line to park and find the plane far up in the sky and follow it until it gently touched the ground in front of us. How do they do it? Late afternoons on the flight-line were exciting and made us proud. The breeze was pleasing, the entertainment was educational and the moment was well remembered. We did and still do feel very attached to Barksdale.

Shreveport has experienced millions of changes over the past most of which I approve — and some I don't — one way streets downtown with which I am constantly bothered! It's all in what you get used to, I guess.

Orvis and I have continued those Sunday treks where the Sherrods left off. We tour our city and are amazed with Youree Drive, residential areas, inner-loops, outer loops and overpasses. We approve of progress when made with much pre-planning and investigation. As a native and a transplant we're here to enjoy Shreveport.

TELEPHONES

Remember when we were in grade school just beginning to learn about American History? Our teachers told us about the Indians who were in this country before the European explorers arrived. The Indians were very unique in many ways especially communicating with smoke signals! We played Cowboy and Indians in my neighborhood but smoke signals? NO!
I personally cannot begin to understand smoke or electricity so I looked up "telephone" -------- forget "mumbo gumbo" and I'll resort to words of my own.

Starting with my "oldest source" he told me his earliest telephone use was on a "crank phone". A 2 foot long box, 10 inches wide, 8 inches deep was attached to the wall. With a receiver and cord hanging from a hook on the left side, the mouthpiece was secured to the center of the box. When visiting my Alabama relatives I was amused at the heights of 4 boxes lined up under the communal phone to accommodate their children. Definite contact had to be made from mouth to mouth piece.

On the right side of the box was a hand crank waiting for the caller to turn. When this happened, bells began to ring and a pleasant and familiar voice who already knew who you were would ask, "Number please?" this could be the introduction to a visit with the operator, her weather report, gossip, or at the very least a connection with the person you were calling. Orvis' phone number was 7558.

These lines were definitely not for one residence but several hence they were referred to as party lines. Each line had a different number of rings – 1-2, etc. Can't you imagine waiting for an important call and counting the rings on your phone?

The first Sherrod phone I remember was described as the "Candlestick Phone", a round base secured a slender candlestick about 10 inches tall with a mouthpiece sitting on top. On the side of the candlestick was a hook holding the receiver. The most admirable quality was that it had a 6 foot card out of the wall connection. Sitting down to talk was a miracle! Our phone number was 75350!

I'll never understand how my Dad conducted railroad business, Mother organized her activities, my sister's friends and when I got old enough for phone use we didn't go nuts waiting for our turn! Sitting in that hall with a 6 ft. line there was definitely no privacy. Every word was absorbed, weighed, and analyzed. They were public information. My friends could hear Mother saying "If you don't get off that phone right now ----!" Their parents were saying the same thing at their end. Life was tough!

Our French cradle phone came next. Construction was simpler. The 5 inch base housed the dial and cradle to hold the receiver, which looked like a small dumbbell. You listened with one end and spoke into the other. I loved it because you could cradle it between your head and shoulder allowing your hands to be free. It's best feature was its 25 ft. cord. If the phone wasn't in the hall one would grab the cord and follow it through the house until it was located. The trip was worth it. Life was good!

At age 10 and 12 Peggy and I decided we needed a private line. We found 2 tin cans, punched small holes in the bottom's center, threaded with a cord and stretched it from her yard to mine. It worked. I listened when Peggy spoke! Try it and let me know!

Hello 2008! I'm using my 3rd phone smaller than my hand with a thousand symbols none of which have I mastered. Where is the one to cook dinner? What I don't understand is "what is so important that you can't wait until you get home to ask your best friend, "What are your plans for today?"

Most importantly phones deliver messages: I made it back to college; we just had a baby; he died last night; this is the nursing home; I love you.

When I die, push a button and pray, "Beam her up, please God".

THANKSGIVING II

Remembering through all my years of Thanksgivings – dinners, people, locations, lessons taught, stories related, school day vacations, once a year songs, leftovers, I still get teary-eyed. Daddy, Mother, Kiki, my sister, and I completed the Sherrod family unit. My thanks started there and remains there.

Today I alone live of the original 5, but I've added 24 more! Orvis, our daughters, in-laws, grandchildren, in-laws, and great-grandchildren with Sherrod and Sigler blood galloping thru healthy and happy bodies. Happy Thanksgiving from us to ALL of you! (I'm cooking for 3!)

Trying to wipe the clouds away, my first Thanksgiving memories are those centered around our dining table with family and friends as Daddy says his blessing which always began with "Our Gracious Heavenly Father." A beautifully set table with turkey et al and Kiki waiting to serve Mother's hot homemade rolls (can't you smell them?) finished the scene.

Following was football, Byrd/Fair Park, games on the big Emerson radio, and with friends in our backyard. What a day – and just think Friday was a holiday and leftovers were over-crowding the ice box. Why die – I was already in heaven.

Barret teachers provided ways of observing these holidays – Monday, Tuesday, and Wednesday. I later realized how thankful teachers were for Thursday and Friday.

My favorite project was to use a cigar box with screen over the top. Place a piece of paper with leaves arranged nicely in the box, dip a toothbrush in colored paint, scratch it across the screen, let it dry, remove the leaves and – an original by little Joanne! Do they still do that?

When Liz and Anne were little their Daddy told them about the original Thanksgiving letting them assume it took place on Red River behind his parent's place. I made costumes for them which Anne referred to as "pildrums." Liz loved riding her horse pretending to be an Indian. Aren't imaginations wonderful?

Friday was also memorable – a day to rake those 3 big trees leaves on William Street. That old-fashioned iron rake was hard to handle. The prize – asking all the Sunny Slope neighbors to bring their straightened coat hangers to roast marshmallows – plenty in the winter and summer for the new rice crispie and marshmallow recipe. Mmm good!

Shreveport is not fond of producing colorful leaves without the right trees. One is Marty's oriental trees are with red leaves all year. Don't miss the blazing yellow leaves Ginko on Sandefur and Tibbs.

If you want a treat to fall, head to the Northeast. From the air and on the street, the bright reds, oranges, yellow and evergreens provide an o-o-ah trip.

Last weekend Liz and I attended my great niece's wedding in Alice, Texas. No leaves there, but I did see pines standing at attention in an assortment of blue-green uniforms and a fire – charred pine making a fall statement. Others included red buck-eyed bush, white bushy goat weed, wild dogwood turning, and typical Christmas trees.

In South Texas, the contrast was a surprise. Amid the oil wells, windmills, Black Angus, and Santa Gertrudis there were mesquite trees, several kinds of cactus and 20 feet tall Royal Palms surveying the flat land which produces Hackberry trees, the only sign of fall with its red leaves – that's it!

As expected Thanksgiving begins in our homes, on our drive back I took introspection. It's a little like "which came first the chicken or the egg?" It starts with people in our early life both "here and there" and the influence each had on our existence. One lead to another and then another – try it. Following individuals come groups of people known and unknown which leads us to the largest collection for whom we should be thankful, loyal, faithful – United States of America! "My native country thee, land of the noble free, thy name I love………Our father's God, to thee, author of liberty, to thee we sing; long may our land be bright with freedom's holy light; protect us by thy might, great God, our King."

                Happy Thanksgiving
                Joanne and Family

TIME CHANGES THINGS

Remember when…. You had your first birthday party? Pictures from mine suggest I was about 4 years old with long black curls and a big bow! Fast forward- today and I'm completely gray- headed which was not brought on by age. I had a few in high school as a result of Ann E. Brown's geometry and trigonometry with Betty McKnight at Centenary.

My gray started the Tuesday after Labor Day 1954 at Longview High School teaching English and Speech. They popped out like Daffodils on Mrs. Fullilove's front yard. The good news is I found a patch of new black hair venturing out last week! Oh happy day there is a God, or hormones or I need new glasses or it's time to remove my cataract. With my luck they'll fall out next Saturday.

Birthdays are the beginning of time measured by years spent with family and friends while enjoying opportunities and experiences, failures and success in our lives.

Mother constantly educated me with her proverbs. Her favorite was "A woman who tells her age will tell you anything!" If you've lived in Shreveport long enough that information is easily accessible by anyone. Find out when she graduated from high school and with 11 or 12 grades of education. But what difference does a total of years of time make anyway? The Bible predicts 3 score and 10. For those of us who have passed that time- God speed!

Her experiences also taught me that after 50 years my hours would start to diminish. Well, I swear I'm down to about 18 a day! What's happened with my Time? I guess it's how you use it.

I asked several friends about favorite birthdays and Judy's is my favorite! It was her 21st in Paris while walking on the Champs-Elysées with friends accompanied by hundreds of Frenchmen celebrating Buzz Aldrin's walk on the moon. People tapped her shoulder and congratulated her with "American on moon" and "A job well done." Time marches on!

My family was discussing birthday parties and gifts, but we/they reached no decisions for my April 2 birthday tonight. No planned party that I know of, I don't desire or want anything special (although April does stand for diamonds)- so hopefully I get cards, hugs, kisses, a phone call from Dot on Cape Cod (it's hers too) or if anyone wants to send money I'll go fill up my car! Today is my 76th Time to celebrate.

      Webster's says: "Time: a nonspatial continuum that is measured in terms of events which succeed one another from past through present to the future." Once we use it up it's gone, but hopefully we get more tomorrow. The only thing I don't like about birthdays is- the older I get- the older my friends get, and that's when we begin to experience loss- but that's life. Since last June many of our friends have reached their Time limit. After having Time out, Time and a half, Time off and overTime. Our heavenly Time keeper keeps check on his Timetable he has for each of us.

      However before that Time we are given instructions from Ecclesiastes 3:1-8. "To everything there is a season and a Time to every purpose under heaven: A Time to be born and a Time to die; a Time to plant and a Time to pluck up that which is planted; a Time to kill, and a Time to heal; a Time to break down, and a Time to build up; a Time to weep, and a Time to laugh; a Time to mourn, and a Time to dance; a Time to cast away stones, and a Time to gather stones together; a Time to embrace, and a Time to refrain from embracing; a Time to get and a Time to lose; a Time to keep, and a Time to cast away; a Time to mend, and a Time to sew; a Time to keep silence, and a Time to speak; a Time to love, and a Time to hate; a Time of war, and a Time of peace."

      Happy Birthday to all and to all a good year.

TREES ARE GOD'S GIFTS

Remember when Spring was on its way or so you thought?

When I looked out of my dining room window on March 7th, I was amazed with the size of beautiful snowflakes drifting down from the sky and resting on the brand new leaves, flowers, and buds of my Bradford Pear tree. That tree has been standing at attention beside my driveway since last fall after letting go of its 2007 crop of leaves. Finally it has gotten up the courage to send out its first announcement of life in 2008 – and it snows! But today March 17th and very fittingly for the date, my Pear tree is full of beautiful green leaves and white blossoms. It appears that the snow had absolutely no affect. On my 65th birthday, April 2, it also snowed – Beware – as I reported earlier, Global Warming and its surprises began in Shreveport – fur coat on swim suit?

Driving around Shreveport is a pleasant chore. Some species of trees send blossoms out presumably to check the weather before their leaves make an appearance. Others do the opposite. The variety of trees in our city is outstanding.

The Ginkgo tree on the corner of Sandefur and Tibbs is my favorite color of green, but in the fall the leaves turn to a beautiful sunshine yellow. The leaves are fan-shaped and wave in the slightest breeze. The encyclopedia stated, "the Ginkgo looks the same as it did thousands of years ago when it grew in ancient times. It can live in today's polluted cities and is being planted in parks and metropolitan areas." Drive by and enjoy.   Of all our trees we Sherrods enjoyed our three pear trees which had once been a part of the Fullilove Orchard. The tornado which traveled down Kings Highway demolished two. The remaining tree provided Mother and Kiki enough to make the best preserves ever. Mitzi and Wanda come in second. Don't know why but don't your taste buds and memory just have a way of telling you if it's like Mother's?

Peggy and I were cautioned constantly about eating green pears. We couldn't resist and we never got sick. Peggy left me a Jade green pear to remember her by.

There was an old Negro man who traveled up William Street frequently. One day he stopped and asked Daddy if he could have the rotten pears on the ground. "What for" questioned Daddy. "I got a pigpen full of pigs that could eat 'em up," he answered with a huge smile. He returned many years in his mule-drawn wagon always giving Peggy and me a ride to Kings Highway. Fun days!

Other trees which Peggy and I relished were our Fig trees. Hers was at the gate between our yards and mine was behind our horse barn. I'll bet no one else took a cereal bowl full of milk to the fig tree and ate breakfast in its shade! Our mothers and Kiki made sure we left enough for preserves – another delicacy from their kitchens.

Of all God's gifts, trees are my favorite. They are a visual joy with their arrangement of naked branches, seasonal leaf colors, height, and fruits. Their competition is never boring!

Sergeant Joyce Kilmer's "Trees" is my favorite:

> "I think that I shall never see
> A poem as lovely as a tree.
> A tree whose hungry mouth is prest
> Against the earth's sweet flowing breast;
> A tree that looks at God all day,
> And lifts her leafy arms to pray;
> A tree that may in summer wear
> A nest of ravens in her hair;
> Upon whose bosom snow has lain;
> Who intimately lives with rain.
> Poems are made by fools like me,
> But only God can make a tree."

For all of you and me.

TRIBUTE FOR OUR VETERANS

My tribute to Monday's Memorial Day follows. A little late but it's always necessary to Remember!

In 2006 Liz, Connor and I had without a doubt the most meaningful experience of our lives. We went to Normandy. As we walked the winding road we discovered thousands of white crosses as if standing in perfect formation for the call to duty. We saw first hand how many men and women are buried there as a result of fighting for the freedom America and other countries have today. We were stunned and stood still with tears in our eyes and hands on our hearts. There was so much emotion in my mind and heart I could not breathe. I felt that I needed to say thanks to each white cross. Suddenly I recalled portions of the poem "In Flanders Field" written by Canadian Lt. Col. John McCrae who died in France in 1918.

"In Flanders Field the posies blow Between the crosses row on row, That mark our place; and in the sky The larks, still bravely singing, fly Scarce heard amid the guns below.

We are the Dead. Short days ago we lived, felt dawn, saw sunset glow, Loved and were loved, and now we lie in Flanders fields.

Take up our quarrel with the foe; To you from failing hands we throw The Torch; be yours to hold it high. If ye break faith with us who die we shall not sleep, though poppies grow In Flanders Fields."

Leaving the cemetery our guide took us to Omaha and Utah beaches. The trenches and bunkers are still embedded in the terrain and history. As ugly as this war was Normandy is a memorial to those who defended it and lost their lives bravely. We will never forget being there.

The summer of 1949 my parents and I drove to New York City and Washington, D.C. Picnicking along the roadside, stopping at historical sites, staying in small motels with garages separating the rooms – What an adventure!

In Washington we toured Arlington National Cemetery where the Tomb of the Unknown Soldier lies. Our visit coincided with their Memorial Day ceremonies with the music of the United States Marine band. The inscription on the tomb reads: "Here lies in honored glory an American soldier known but to God." Standing atop that hill my panoramic view included white crosses, Washington's

Monument, the Mall, reflecting pools and rested on the United States Capital. With deep emotion for the fallen warriors and feeling so proud of being an American I could hardy stand still as the band played our National Anthem.

Not all soldiers die on battlefields. Our VA hospitals are full of those brave souls. My favorite Marine Robbie Robinson suffered frostbite on his lower legs and feet in the 1952 Korean Conflict. On returning to Shreveport he led an active life even after his legs were
amputated. His leadership of the Boy Scout troop at St. Marks proved beneficial to many boys. Ask their parents today.

In the late 90's he called and asked me to visit him at Schumpert Hospital. We've been friends since Barret School so I was at a loss as to what to expect. When I arrived his wife was there and Robbie said "get in the bed, I'm cold." Vi laughed and gave her permission. (I had on jeans!) "Jo Jo," he said, "Would you be one of my pallbearers?" Answer: "Robbie, you are too bad to die." We laughed, and I accepted.

A month later the expected call came. I put on my black suit and joined his other friends as we followed his casket down St. Mark's aisle. I realized that this act is the most wonderful compliment a friend can ask of a friend – to be together until the end.

Arriving in Forest Park, we carried Robbie to his last post, placed our lapel flowers beside him and stood quietly while from Irv Selber's trumpet we listened to "Taps" from the overlooking hill: "Thanks and praise, for our days, 'neath the sun, 'neath the stars, 'neath the sky; As we go, this we know, God is nigh.

TRIPS TO GROCERY STORE

Remember when you were about 10 years old, playing peacefully in the backyard with friends and your Mother called you inside? I thought, what did she catch me doing this time, and where was my Kiki? They were cooking and discovered a recipe ingredient was missing from the cabinet. Daddy had the car, and the next set of wheels belonged to me!

"Wash your hands, put on your sandals, and go to the store." Each friend ran home asking permission to accompany me and probably was given a list and money, also. Destination – the A&P on the Southern Avenue and Wilkinson Streets corner.

We rode those bicycles as fast as possible because we needed to return to "our work:" climbing trees, sandbox castles, marbles, or telling secrets. "A child's work is never done!"
With luck we ended up with an extra nickel for a drink. In my case – Dr. Pepper, 10-2-4 didn't matter then – doesn't matter now.

Mother's serious shopping took place at Fairfield Big Chain, quite an adventure. Ed Wile produced a grocery chain, this being the first, which attracted every woman in and around Shreveport. Of course, it was closed on Sundays, but the other six days it was thriving. His sister operated a small bookstore just inside the front door and always greeted customers with a smile. If I got restless Mother sent me to find a book to buy.

The chocolate éclairs were to die for along with everything else in the bakery. The vegetables and fruits were the freshest and shelves were neat. The clientele was varied and Mr. Wile spoke to each, giving the store a warm and welcoming feeling. We didn't go there for a loaf of bread – but for serious shopping and visiting experience.

At 25, still living at home, I married and entered a new world. After the honeymoon I found myself in quite a dilemma. What had I said "I do" to? I knew I was obligated to clean and other chores but with teaching school and Ben's cotton farming schedule which demanded attention from sun-up to sun-down, I realized I was in trouble. I had to cook supper, which had a prerequisite of a trip to the grocery store! Dear God – what have I done to myself? (Those of you reading this must be chuckling and remembering!)

I was forced to stock my entire kitchen cabinets with EVERYTHING! (By 29 I was completely gray!) Anything that's connected with food outside of a restaurant sends me into orbit. My kitchen window houses a sign given to me by Lila, "Cooking makes you ugly" – that's my excuse so please forgive me.

I've had scads of grocery store experiences of varying degrees. When Liz, Anne, and I married Orvis, Steve, and Sally I turned into a nervous wreck everyday at 3:00. Preparing dinner every night until they all grew up and left our table was a challenge, and I was glad and already gray!

Thankfully Brookshires was only 6 blocks down Fern – until it closed! I hated those Brookshires Brothers, but I do remember fun times there. Mr. Woods the manager constantly placed unwanted items in my basket and told Marie to tell the other checkers loudly "Look what Mrs. Sigler bought!" Snuff, adult diapers, red hair dye just to name a few.

86 years old Orvis related his first visits to the grocery store in his youth. His mother called in her list which was to be picked up later or delivered. Meats were cut to the customer's preference and refrigerated. It was a customer – pleasing operation. Gone are the days!

Recalling customers reminds me of my parents. Not wanting to offend any store their retirement schedule allowed shopping at Brookshires on the weekends and Weingartens across the street during the week – always wonderfully attired.

My UpTown Brookshires visit to purchase 3 items yesterday took 1 hour. Had wonderful visits with friends especially Dempsy whose son John, an employee of 32 years, knows where everything is. So does manager, Don Webster whom I taught as an eighth grader.

I realize the "toll" is expensive and unavoidable but necessary for life. Who needs a country club? Just go grocery shopping and have a nice day.

TROLLEY TRAVEL

Remember when we rode the Shreveport trolleys all over town? They were the most efficient method of covering the city on wheels. For students it only cost 7¢ and that could include a transfer to another trolley. I wouldn't be surprised to learn that a passenger could travel the entire system on one regular priced ticket, asking for a transfer repeatedly while riding on the Line Avenue, Brooadmoor, Highland, Queensbourough, Cedar Grove and Crosstown lines.

Of course these vehicles were not air-conditioned but powered by electric lines attached to "over the street" cables. These were great temptations during Halloween trick or treat season as teenagers loved stopping traffic because of a disconnected trolley.

Trolley stops probably were at every other block intersection and easily visible. Taylor reminded me of the antenna symbols attached to the front top of the trolley. These could be seen easily so that the wait in the weather – good or bad could be endured – all this for 7¢!

As I waited for the light to change at the top of the hill intersection of Line and Jordan I decided to reminisce. Jordan can be confusing to newcomers because Shreveporters, while reading the Bible, say Jordan but while reading the phone books say Jerdon!

As I glanced back to the right I could see in my mind's eye the stately white brick home of the Herold family. Torn down several years ago I cursed progress under my breath!

I decided to test myself and compare "today with yesterday" down Line Avenue.

Dr. Stamper's house and later his hospital and medical office building were great additions to the medical scene at that intersection.

On the Margaret Street/Herndon corners are two landmarks. To the right is the Women's Department Club where many cultural events are held. Across Line is the Agudath Achim Synagogue.

Down a block was the Line Avenue Grade School with its cylinder 2-story fire escape attached to the building. A circular slide provided safe and a fun adventure while avoiding a possible fire – how clever.

On the corner of Olive was a beautiful 2-story home belonging to the Hicks or Kobler family with its name Belmore Place written on the brick gate columns. When I entered Kindergarten I met Belmore Hicks the granddaughter of the owners of Belmore Place.

The fire station at the corner of Wilkinson and Line was a wonderful destination for our Barrett School classes to visit on beautiful sunny days. The visit I remember most was when I took my grandson Scott at 3 to see the fire trucks up close. It was over powering to him – especially when the fireman honked the horn!

Columbia Park on the left represented numerous birthday parties for me and my girls, although the swings and slides didn't compare to Betty Virginia's.

I still get a chill when I stop at the Line and Kings Highway corner. I was baptized and the first bride in the chapel of this beautiful church. Full of Christian symbolisms I can still hear Mother's voice singing wonderful hymns.

Diagonally is the city of Byrd where I spent five years of my education. It provides me with memories of dedicated teachers, wonderful friends, hours of homework, outstanding activities, my children's education, and present-day opportunities to "keep the hive alive."

The next block of Line between Gladstone and Stephenson was quite busy. At 3:00 half the student body appeared at the filling station buying cokes at Glenwood Drugstore ordering an Idiots Delight or hamburgers, or across the street at Darrel's Grill sharing a chocolate soda. I can still taste them!

Also included were Baird's Ladies shop, a bicycle shop, Sue Peyton's and best of all the Glenwood Theatre where I "experienced" my first viewing of "Gone With the Wind."

Traveling on Line is ingrained in me – couldn't do without it. We all have our paths of importance. Some might be straight and narrow, but thankfully they criss-cross with others.

Say what you please about remembering people, places, and events. The past will always impact our future actions. We must appreciate the influence they have made on our lives because "no man is an island."

VALENTINE'S DAY

Remember the school days of the 30s and 40s? There weren't many holidays, but one was very special – Valentine's Day. We weren't aware of its origin but later learned that it was named after 2 saints named Valentine centuries ago in Rome. It's unknown why they are associated with messages of love. That being said Valentine Day is fun and red.

Daddy always presented Mother with a box of Russel Stover chocolate candy. It came in a sturdy yellow box of 2 layers of pieces wrapped in brown to match the chocolate and gold/silver. Mother would ration that candy to us which probably lasted until Easter. When we cleaned my parents home out for them to go to the "retirement home," I found about a dozen boxes saved with "things" in them because they were nice little storage boxes. Daddy was always safe with a beautiful Valentine and a Stover box.

Mother loved to write poems so I don't know if this is original. I've heard it all my life and taught it to my children and grandchildren. "If you love me like I love you, no knife can cut our love in two." I wrote this poem on the lap blanket I made for Mother to be used in her "retirement home." We read it together on each visit.

Valentine versus probably began with "Roses are Red, Violets are Blue, Sugar is sweet and so are you." Everyone has used that poem as a guide and applied our own wit and words of love.

Lila reminded me that in our first grade at BARRET we made valentines out of red construction paper and white doilies. Our teacher Miss Sweat placed decorated sacks with our names on them in the chalk and eraser tray of the blackboard. Playing post office, we mailed our cards as we walked around the room. It was exciting to see who sent them and what the verse was. The room – mothers brought punch and cookies and those tiny colored hearts with messages of I love you, Be mine, Kiss me, etc which are still popular today. Years later Lila taught at BARRET and celebrated the tradition of hand-made cards. "If it ain't broke, don't fix it"

Patsy's South Highland's memories are of shoe boxes (tops and bottoms) decorated red and white with glitter. These were individual mail boxes so I assume they were the beginning of the game "Post Office." Ask an old person for the definition!

Orvis's family owned a drugstore which he remembered sold valentines for 1¢ or a package of 12 for 10¢. Two of the boxed candies sold were Pangburns and Russel Stover. Other companies' candy was in red heart shaped boxes which also were saved by girls. What a lovely gift for the one you love! (HINT) with a sweet valentine message! (HINT)

For some reason Orvis and I have always sought out funny cards for each other, but every now and then I get a serious one which I love. I always get dinner out (make reservations) because I hate to cook. Here's a poem you might use, "Violets are blue, Roses are red, if you want dinner take us out to be fed."
Valentines are not only for man and wife, boy, and girl etc. Just go to the store and Hallmark will fill your list.

Mother always had a twinkle in her eye and sometimes I should not have asked why. One Valentine day she composed a short poem for me which I didn't appreciate. On the back side of her lap blanket I wrote it to see if she remembered it. When she saw it we laughed and reminisced about the good old days. "I love you little, I love you big, I love you like a little pig."
Or how about Elizabeth Barrett Browning's sonnet 43 which begins , "How do I love thee? Let me count the ways"…and ends— "I love thee with the breath, smiles, tears of all my life – and, if God choose, I shall but love thee better after death."

Happy Valentine's to each of you.

VOLUNTEERISM

Remember when August was coming to an end and your mother begins to smile again? If I was too young to be interested in the calendar I knew by the twinkle in my Edith Bunker – type Mother's eyes that something wonderful was going to happen. That smile seemed to rub off on Daddy and Kiki. By the third grade I finally wised up! I might have been dumb, but I wasn't stupid! August, September, Labor Day – oh my goodness, school will be starting on Tuesday! (Editors note: As always we of the older generation don't understand all those unnecessary holidays. Why not just enjoy Thanksgiving, Christmas, and Good Friday? With no air conditioning we were thrilled to get cool-weather holidays and then summer on May 31st. Try it School Board, you might like it.)

I attended only three schools in my sixteen year education process. Seven at Barret, five at Byrd, and four at Centenary, and I have to admit I loved school and all it stood for. Those of you who know me well are probably thinking – yes before 8:00, at lunch, between classes, and after 3:00, and especially attending the extra curricular activities – and you are right.

In the Dark Ages at Barret our after school activities were limited to Girl/Brownie Scouts' and Boy/Cub Scouts' meetings. By the time we arrived at high school the number of activities had greatly enlarged! Our athletes practiced after school as did our special interest clubs. The sponsors of these clubs were dedicated to their purpose yet approached the members in such a way that the club equaled the enthusiasm of the student.

To illustrate: The Red Cross Club at Byrd, sponsored by Celia Smiley, "offered the opportunity to serve at home and abroad in peace and war between schools and the circle of local, national, and international society". This was quite admirable however the membership also planned the Red Cross Assembly which was always looked forward to by the students.

Miss Smiley allowed very little monkey business, but my senior year she proved herself full of it by allowing the club to re-write "Mac Beth" which she taught with great enthusiasm. From using a metal garbage can top to represent Mac Beth's shield to a #3 washtub full of bubbling hot ice for a caldron, Mac Beth came to life and was finally understood by resistant students of Shakespeare. The students loved it and couldn't wait to join the Red Cross Club – yeah! (Years later one of the players became president of the Advisory Red Cross Board!) Time spent by the membership included visiting hospitals, packing and shipping gift boxes overseas and sponsoring and running the First Aid Room at the school.

My point in writing about the extra curricular undertaking is to find what challenges are inside our hearts and minds, no matter what we are – age, sex, color, or national origin it's referred to as volunteering. "One who acts on one's free will without valuable consideration or legal obligation with cheerful consent and willing heart" says Webster.

Schools and teachers have a great influence on helping to create a student's character and philosophy. That's were volunteerism is first taught without being obvious.
Borrowing Anna's Broadmoor Magnet yearbook, I found their extra curricular activities included. 4H, Building Urban Gardens by Students, the oldest Junior Red Cross Club in Junior High in Louisiana, N.A.S.A., A.R.T., Edisonian, music clubs, and athletics.

The Byrd Gusher disclosed varied activities plus many more which independence and transportation provide.

Regardless of the type of school, it is a CITY. Classrooms are the student's jobs, principals and teachers are their leaders, learning to live with them and students from 8-3:00 five days a week prepares them for the outside world which will face them at 18 years of age. Their ability to learn and absorb for 12 years is incredible. As students we are taught so much without realizing it. Surfacing years later we're thankful we paid attention.
School-taught, volunteerism leads to membership on advisory Boards of medical, educational cultural, religious, government, alumni, corporate, and special interest organizations all filled by men and women "who cheerfully give their time – with a willing heart without obligation! Sign up! and encourage others to be a good example!

About the Author

   Joanne Sherrod Sigler is a life long native and booster of Shreveport, Louisiana. Growing up in the Sunny Slope Subdivision of Shreveport, Joanne attended neighborhood schools gathering life long friends and a wealth of memories.
   Widowed with two daughters at a young age, Joanne went on to marry , Orvis Sigler, enlarging her friend circle. The marriage brought his two daughters and a son to her family.
   The busy life of a wife, community volunteer and mother delayed Joanne's writing career. Fortunately for the reader, Joanne is making up for lost time. This is her second book, the first being "Love Returned, a Daughters Journey" the story of her struggles with the care of aging parents.
   Stay tuned, there will be more to follow.